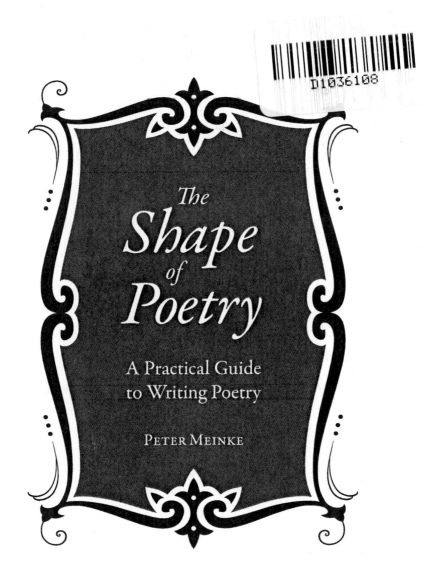

The
Shape
of
Poetry

A Practical Guide
to Writing Poetry

PETER MEINKE

jefferson
press

PERMISSION

Adrian, Vonna, "A Plaguey Thing," from *A Gaggle of Verses*, Bits Press, copyright © 1986, 1988 by Vonna Adrian. Reprinted by permission.

Auden, W.H., "Have a Good Time," from *Collected Shorter Poems*, Vintage Books, Random House; reprinted by permission of the publisher.

Baker, David, "Sonnet for a Separation"; this poem appeared in *The Chariton Review*, and is reprinted by permission of the author, copyright © by David Baker.

Gibbons, Reginald, "Lemon Trees," reprinted by permission of the author, copyright © by Reginald Gibbons.

Gioia, Dana, "My Confessional Sestina," reprinted by permission of the author, from *The Gods of Winter*, Graywolf Press, copyright © 1991 by Dana Gioia.

Hollander, Jean, "Habits of Love," reprinted by permission of the author, copyright © by Jean Hollander.

Kennedy, X.J., "B Negative," from *Cross Ties: Selected Poems*, reprinted by permission of the author, copyright © 1996 by X.J. Kennedy.

Kumin, Maxine, "Night Soil," from *House, Bridge, Fountain, Gate*, copyright © 1975 by Maxine Kumin, reprinted by permission of the author.

Lautermilch, Steven, from "Petals on a Burning Pond," by permission of the author, Hour Press Chapbook, Kill Devil Hills, NC, copyright © 1997 by Steven Lautermilch.

All the poems by Peter Meinke are reprinted by permission of the author and the University of Pittsburgh Press as follows:

"The Golden Bird," from *The Night Train and The Golden Bird*, copyright © 1977 by Peter Meinke.

"Miss Arbuckle," "Recipe," and "Teacups," from *Trying to Surprise God*, copyright © 1981 by Peter Meinke.

"A Dream of Third Base" and "The Shells of Bermuda," from *Night Watch* on the *Chesapeake*, copyright © 1987 by Peter Meinke.

"The ABC of Aerobics," "Atomic Pantoum," "Dear Reader," "The Heart's Location," "In Gentler Times," "Lines from Neuchatel," "Liquid Paper," "Plovers," "Rage," "Soldiers with Green Leggings," "Talk of the Paintings," "Teaching Poetry at a Country School in Florida," and "To a Daughter with Artistic Talent," from *Liquid Paper: New & Selected Poems*, copyright © 1991 by Peter Meinke.

ISBN: 9780977808656
Library of Congress Control Number: 2008925567

jefferson
press
808 Scenic Highway
Lookout Mountain, TN 37350

THE SHAPE OF POETRY

A Practical Guide to Writing Poetry

by PETER MEINKE

Publishers   The Writer, Inc.   *Boston*

Permissions

Adrian, Vonna, "A Plaguey Thing," from *A Gaggle of Verses*, Bits Press, copyright © 1986, 1988 by Vonna Adrian. Reprinted by permission.

Auden, W.H., "Have a Good Time," from *Collected Shorter Poems*, Vintage Books, Random House; reprinted by permission of the publisher.

Baker, David, "Sonnet for a Separation"; this poem appeared in *The Chariton Review*, and is reprinted by permission of the author, copyright © by David Baker.

Gibbons, Reginald, "Lemon Trees," reprinted by permission of the author, copyright © by Reginald Gibbons.

Gioia, Dana, "My Confessional Sestina," reprinted by permission of the author, from *The Gods of Winter*, Graywolf Press, copyright © 1991 by Dana Gioia.

Hollander, Jean, "Habits of Love," reprinted by permission of the author, copyright © by Jean Hollander.

Kennedy, X. J., "B Negative," from *Cross Ties: Selected Poems*, reprinted by permission of the author, copyright © 1996 by X. J. Kennedy.

Kumin, Maxine, "Night Soil," from *House, Bridge, Fountain, Gate*, copyright © 1975 by Maxine Kumin, reprinted by permission of the author.

Lautermilch, Steven, from "Petals on a Burning Pond," by permission of the author, Hour Press Chapbook, Kill Devil Hills, NC, copyright © 1997 by Steven Lautermilch.

All the poems by Peter Meinke are reprinted by permission of the author and the University of Pittsburgh Press, as follows:

"The Golden Bird," from *The Night Train and the Golden Bird*, copyright © 1977 by Peter Meinke.

"Miss Arbuckle," "Recipe," and "Teacups," from *Trying to Surprise God*, copyright © 1981 by Peter Meinke.

"A Dream of Third Base" and "The Shells of Bermuda," from *Night Watch on the Chesapeake*, copyright © 1987 by Peter Meinke.

"The ABC of Aerobics," "Atomic Pantoum," "Dear Reader," "The Heart's Location," "In Gentler Times," "Lines from Neuchatel," "Liquid Paper," "Plovers," "Rage," "Soldiers with Green Leggings," "Talk of the Paintings," "Teaching Poetry at a Country School in Florida," and "To a Daughter with Artistic Talent," from *Liquid Paper: New & Selected Poems*, copyright © 1991 by Peter Meinke.

"Black Holes & Einstein," "Blow, Blow, Thou Winter Wind," "Goalfish," "Ice," "Noreen," "The Olive Garden," "The Secret Code," and "Warpath," from *Scars*, copyright © 1996 by Peter Meinke.

Library of Congress Cataloging-in-Publication Data

Meinke, Peter.
  The shape of poetry / by Peter Meinke.
    p. cm.
  Includes bibliographical references (p.).
  ISBN 0-87116-186-9
  1. Poetry—Authorship. I. Title.
  PN1059.A9M45 1999
  808.1—dc21

99-13050
CIP

ACKNOWLEDGMENTS

I want to thank all the poets, writers and editors quoted here in bits and snippets for the pleasure and privilege of reading their work over the years. They are the ground on which we stand.

I especially want to thank Ed Ochester, Cynthia Miller and the University of Pittsburgh Press for allowing me to quote so amply from books of mine that they have published.

Thanks also to Anna Bourgeois, Christine Kandaouroff, and the directors of Le Chateau de Lavigny (Switzerland) for providing a stay at the Chateau in the summer of 1998, during which time this manuscript was completed.

And special thanks to Sylvia K. Burack and Anne Rimbey for reading this manuscript, and for their helpful comments and suggestions.

This book is for all my students, past and present, with gratitude and affection.

Contents

And, as imagination bodies forth
The forms of things unknown, the poet's pen
Turns them to shapes, and gives to airy nothing
A local habitation and a name.

—William Shakespeare, from *A Midsummer*
  Night's Dream

Sweet are the pleasures that to verse belong,
And doubly sweet a brotherhood in song.

—John Keats, from "To John Felton Mathew"

THE SHAPE OF POETRY

Introduction

The Shape of Poetry has been written with half an eye on the millennium coming up. My *Oxford English Dictionary*'s third definition of "millennium" is "a period of happiness and benign government"—a good description of how we feel when we're writing well. And the fourth definition of "shape" in my *Webster's II* has to do with the "condition in which something may exist or appear"—as in the state of poetry today, as well as the other obvious meanings about the shape of individual poems. So the first lesson here is to keep a couple of good dictionaries, learn the various meanings of words, and use whichever ones best suit your purpose.

> "The question is," said Alice, "whether you *can* make words mean so many different things."
> "The question is," said Humpty Dumpty, "which is to be master—that's all."

The text that follows is designed to make you more like Humpty Dumpty. No one said poetry has to be safe.

* * *

This is a book about writing poetry. *Being* a poet isn't important, but *writing* poetry is. This may sound paradoxical, but I've met many would-be poets who weren't very much interested in actually writing or reading poems.

One problem with writing a book like this is that every single piece of advice by itself sounds specious, be-

3

cause poetry, like life, is multi-faceted. As soon as you describe it one way, the opposite seems to be true. For example, if I had said that poetry was "single-minded" instead of "multi-faceted," it would have made just as much sense, looked at from another angle. So my advice is, for writing poetry and in reading this book, *be patient* and the right words will fall into the right places: "Ripeness is all," saith the Bard.

I had an uncle who could write funny and sentimental poems on demand at birthday parties or weddings, and then jump up on a table and recite them. But even when I first began to feel that strange itch to write down beautiful words, I knew instinctively that I wanted to be a different kind of poet. I was—and remain—too slow a writer to produce a poem on immediate demand; and if by accident I could have, I was too shy to recite it. My poetry seemed to well up in some murky part of my psyche—the uncensored and politically incorrect part. For example, after World War II, I was, among other things, intrigued by the Japanese soldiers who were said to be still hiding on Guam and the other islands where the bloody battles took place:

> Deep in the tropical jungle where
> green light filtered through vine and palm
> an elderly soldier will not surrender . . .

The fact that I had scarcely seen a tree, much less a jungle, didn't bother me a bit as I set poems and stories in the South Pacific, complete with lizards, shellfish, and coconuts. (Five decades later, things have reversed. I sit here in St. Petersburg, Florida, surrounded by beaches, and write about Brooklyn—an illustration of what Edgar Allan Poe called "the imp of the perverse.") Young writers are always told, "Write about what you know," so perhaps an early lesson of this book should be: *Be skeptical of all generalities.* It makes basic sense to write about something you're familiar with, but sometimes you should just write because you feel like it, you're compelled to, you want to see how something sounds. Poets aren't reporters, at least not in the obvious way.

I think all young people are attracted to poetry—who hasn't written poems in his or her youth?—but that attraction is snuffed out by schools that don't know how to handle it, parents who don't respect it, and peers who make fun of it. All of this is understandable—what a lot of drivel is written!—but sad, from various angles.

In my case, I became—wrongly, I think—a kind of closet poet, reading and writing each night in my room, not telling or showing anyone except a few teachers who I guessed would be sympathetic. This practice has stayed with me all my life: I seldom show my poems to anyone but an editor until after they've been published. (Josephine Jacobsen does the same thing, calling poetry "an immensely private operation.") This is fine now that I know what I want to do, more or less, but most beginning poets will save time and avoid mistakes if they can find someone whose opinion they value with whom to share their early drafts.

In America, at least, if you want to write poetry, nobody will stop you; if you want to print it, no one will break up your press; if you want to distribute it, you won't be knocked on the head and arrested. But we are also a macho and materialistic society, in which poetry tends to be ignored, if not held in actual contempt. Although a growing number of small—often *very* small—magazines devote themselves to poetry, reviews of poetry books are disappearing from our newspapers. Tiny poetry sections cower in the dusty corners of most bookstores behind phalanxes of best sellers about our health.

Serious poetry is seriously marginalized. At the same time, despite this truth, more people are writing poetry and listening to poetry, and even buying poetry books than ever before.

It's hard for an American poet to sustain an intense belief in the centrality of poetry to our lives—though I believe it's true. What poets do is of the utmost importance. Fortunately, in a country as huge as ours, 265 million people, you're bound to find sympathetic souls if you persist, look sharp, and reach out.

Poetry is important because poets keep our language fresh and honest. Our primary job is to say what we think and feel, and say it well, not to sell something or push some political agenda. This is why in authoritarian countries poets are often the first to get censored.

In an article on "The Language of Poetry," Kenneth Koch wrote that "Poetry lasts because it gives the ambiguous and ever-changing pleasure of being both a statement and a song." Growing up in blue-collar Flatbush, with a strong Brooklyn accent, I became fascinated early on with the music of words. I can remember rolling in my mouth exotic words (woids!) like "vanilla" (which I pronounced "vaniller"), "Managua," "tawny port" (a drink favored by one of my aunts), even "Bronx," which sounded evil to me, probably because the hated Yankees were there. I somehow knew even then, without being able to articulate it, that sounds had meaning.

Poetry feeds the imagination, the most generous of our faculties, the one increasingly important in a multi-everything world. In a paradox that poets should love, our world expands as it shrinks. The smaller it becomes, the more we're aware of other people, places, cultures. Poetry unites us because it is, among other things, the art of seeing similarities rather than differences. Our first critic, Aristotle, observed that the essence of poetry is metaphor: My love is like a rose, the rose is a star, the star an oasis . . . in an unending series of comparisons that eventually, like so many poetic forms, brings us back to our beginnings.

In our best moments, when we think of others instead of ourselves, we still turn to poetry—weddings, births, graduations, deaths—but we would have more best moments if poetry were woven into the fabric of our lives. I was lucky because my mother kept collections of poetry around the house, including Oscar Williams's then-popular anthologies and a beautiful large edition of Whitman's *Leaves of Grass*. I can still feel its rough-textured cover in my hands.

I also had another necessary ingredient in the development of a writer: the occasional teacher who encouraged my efforts, which I would slip in with my papers, sometimes in place of the paper I was supposed to write. Poets don't need a lot of encouragement, but they need *some*. Every poet I know remembers some teachers who helped at just the right time. To this day, I can recite their names: Miss McDermott, Miss Phelan, Miss Nast, Mrs. Vanderbilt. The last, Mrs. Vanderbilt, I particularly liked because she'd respond with humor and creativity, without lowering her strict standards.

One morning, she surprised us with a test on the essays of Charles Lamb, which I hadn't read. (I read constantly, but hardly ever anything that was assigned.) So, hoping she'd let me off the hook for my cleverness, I wrote, *I dislike Lamb / In fact, I shun him / As for his essays / I haven't done 'em,* and turned it in. When the papers came back the next day, she had written in her precise hand, *You have my sympathy / for your antipathy / But there'll be Lamb / on your exam—* followed by a small but very distinct "F."

Of all the teachers I had through grade school and

high school, these are the only four I remember with any clarity. To my real embarrassment (though I must have been inwardly pleased), they often read my poems out loud to the class. So even though my public school career centered on "wholesome" activities like football and baseball, my high school yearbook "prediction" went like this: *Wants to be: Writer. Probably will be: Censored.* I didn't believe it for a minute, but it came true, both parts.

This book is meant to encourage *you*, at all levels. Writing poems is a worthwhile activity. It's good to write them for yourself, "to see what you feel." It's good to write them for others, to communicate these feelings to the people you love. And it's good to publish them, extending that communication to a broader society.

Some critics and writers fear that too much poetry is being written today, that standards are slipping, that the bad drives out the good. I disagree with this: It's like the Mandarin Chinese trying to keep their language from spreading so they could control it. We can't have too much poetry. Bad poems don't drive out good ones, though they can slip into vacuums where there's no poetry at all.

Talent for writing poetry is given, and can't be taught, though talent shows on many different levels and no one agrees on exactly what it is. And whatever agreement we do find is often undone by history. Witness the lists of British Poet Laureates (Laurence Eusden? Nahum Tate?) or American Pulitzer Prize winners (George Dillon? Audrey Wurdemann?).

But part of poetry writing is craft, and almost everyone can be helped in some way. Musicians, artists, actors have to learn their crafts, and so do poets. It's good to remember that Shelley's passionate cry in "To a Skylark" for "profuse strains of unpremeditated art" is written in a premeditated formal style, with a series of triple rhymes that could be achieved only by practice, study, and much rewriting.

This book is aimed at giving you workable suggestions that might save you time, enable you to look at your poems in different ways, recognize your strengths and weaknesses, and, finally, write the best poetry of which you're capable. The givens—which only the individual poet can bring to his or her work—are a passion for poetry and the desire to write it to the highest reaches of one's ability. I'd like this book to amuse, interest, and challenge those readers who stay the course, and I'd like it to help some of you in your efforts to write poems. I think those in the profession—the calling—of writing poetry should be knowledgeable and skilled as any carpenter, passionate and dignified as any priest. I believe those who are able to spend large stretches of their lives engaged in this activity are the luckiest people in the world.

PART ONE: BACKGROUND

ℬ. 1

What Makes Good Poetry?

"WHAT MAKES good poetry?" is one of those subjects that makes me (and most poets) groan. It's amorphous, subjective, and potentially endless. But like many vague questions, it *does* force you to think and take a stand; in fact, several stands, as the "answers" lean against each other like overlapping tiles. It's an important question, one that we're constantly deciding upon as we pick up and put down poems, choose what books of poetry to buy out of the unlimited choices, and tell our friends, "You have to read *this!*"

A serious and talented young writer asked, "How can you tell when a poem is *really* good?," the unspoken corollary question being, "How can we make our own poems better?"

Although everyone has thought about this, most people tend to answer along the lines of "I know it when I read it." This may be true, but is unhelpful because intelligent and sophisticated people like different poems and different poets. Many readers admire John Ashbery, Howard Nemerov, Gwendolyn Brooks, Charles Simic, Maya Angelou, language poets, new formalists—make any random list—but few admire them all. A taste for Ashbery's poetry, for example, might preclude a liking for

Angelou's. So, unless we just believe that good poetry is the kind we write ourselves, it could be helpful for us to use whatever definition we come up with as a way to measure the poems we're working on.

Our tastes are "set" when we're very young, by the first poems that moved us, by our first real teachers (academic or not). Nevertheless, it seems to me that we can make some useful observations on this subject, even though we may not agree on how to apply them. I've broken my definition of good poetry into six intertwining parts, as follows:

A. E. Housman wrote, "Experience has taught me, when I am shaving of a morning, to keep watch over my thoughts, because, if a line of poetry strays into my memory, my skin bristles so that the razor ceases to act." We've all had the experience of being bowled over (goosebumps, tears, laughter, gasps) from reading or hearing a poem. But a truly good poem is as good, or better, upon rereading.

Unlike novels or even short stories, our favorite poems are those we read over and over again. "Age cannot wither her, nor custom stale/Her infinite variety," as Enobarbus said of Cleopatra. This suggests something about the nature of poetry: 1) *It withholds something from us at first,* yielding its secrets slowly. In our poems, it's always a mistake to tell too much, to supply "answers." A poem isn't a sermon or a lecture. "Let us go then, you and I," is the beginning of T. S. Eliot's "The Love Song of J. Alfred Prufrock." Who is "you"? Who is "I"? After all this time, after a million readings, scholars still disagree.

I think a good poem performs two opposite functions at once: 2) *It surprises and satisfies.* Without both of these qualities, a poem either doesn't work, or doesn't work *for long*. (I take for granted that one aspect of good poems is that they *repay* this rereading.)

A poem can surprise in many different ways. It can surprise by vocabulary: "Buffalo Bill's / defunct / who used to / ride a watersmooth-silver / stallion" (E. E. Cummings). Or by image: "Dumb / As old medallions to the thumb" (Archibald MacLeish). Or by idea: "My little horse must think it queer / To stop without a farmhouse near/Between the woods and frozen lake / The darkest evening of the year" (Robert Frost). Or even by punctuation: "The Heart asks Pleasure—first— / And then— Excuse from Pain— / And then—those little Anodynes / That deaden suffering—" (Emily Dickinson).

But after the surprise, *a good poem also seems inevitable*. A typical reaction, expressed in various ways, is, "I knew that, but didn't know I knew it." You don't learn from poetry the way you do from geography (the capital of Costa Rica is San Jose) or history (the battle of Blenheim was fought in 1704). Rather, poetry satisfies an inner sensibility linked to that early-formed "taste," which, though varying from reader to reader, is real and particular.

This feeling of inevitability is connected to the poem's music, its interesting sounds. 3) *A good poem sounds special,* either melodious like T. S. Eliot's, homespun like Robert Frost's, jumpy like William Carlos Williams's, intense like Emily Dickinson's. A poem sets up a rhythm. The insouciant in-your-face tone of "Buffalo Bill's/ defunct" is matched by its ending: "how do you like your blueeyed boy/Mister Death." The hint of formal rhythms in the beginning of "Prufrock" culminates in the iambic pentameter of its last lines:

We have lingered in the chambers of the sea
By sea-girls wreathed with seaweed red and brown
Till human voices wake us, and we drown.

Emily Dickinson's off-rhymes ("Pain," "suffering") in the first stanza lead to the even more jarring conclusion that leaves us hanging in several ways:

And then—to go to sleep—
And then—if it should be
The will of its Inquisitor
The privilege to die—

And Frost's problem in "Stopping By Woods"—how to end his stanzas of triple rhymes, with one unrhymed line—is solved by his repeating his last line: "And miles to go before I sleep, / And miles to go before I sleep," making a quadruple rhyme and a perfect stop. As writers, we have to learn to follow the poem's music and hope that the sense comes along. When Wallace Stevens begins, "Chieftain Iffucan of Azcan in caftan / of tan with henna hackles, halt!," we know he's drunk on the delights of sound, not sense (though it *does* make sense, sort of).

"Follow the music and not the meaning" is a good directive when you're rewriting your poems. It will hardly ever be your idea that's original. If anything, it will be your voice. Sonnets by William Shakespeare, John Donne, William Wordsworth, Robert Frost, Edna St. Vincent Millay, Richard Wilbur, or Rita Dove don't sound at all alike, even though they might have the exact same subjects, rhyme schemes, and number of syllables.

4) *A good poem is memorable.* It becomes part of our mental/emotional landscape, with every line we remember changing us. Reworking your own poems, you should try to make each line memorable. Why should anyone read this? Why should anyone read this *twice*? John Donne was the first one to affect me that way: "Come live with me, and be my love," "She, she is dead; she's dead," "For God's sake hold your tongue, and let me love." I

wanted to memorize (and did) line after line. This, by the way, is one advantage of formal poetry. It's easier to memorize than free verse.

5) *Poems speak to the unanswerable questions.* By moving primarily through images rather than logical constructions, poems address the mystery of existence: Why are we here, who am I, what's true or false, what makes the good life? These are the important questions, and the very act of asking them is as close to a definitive answer as we're likely to get. This is why even people who dislike poetry embrace it at the major turnings of their lives, to celebrate or mourn.

This doesn't mean a poem has to be murky or unfathomable. Rather it means—like that rare phenomenon, a clear and pure lake—a good poem has depth. A strange attribute of "clear" poems like "Stopping by Woods on a Snowy Evening" or William Carlos Williams's "A Red Wheelbarrow" is that they're less clear on rereading, i.e., they can go in so many directions that all kinds of "meanings" are suggested. A good poem, far from being meaningless, tends to have many meanings. Even a simple love poem means something different to a high school girl, a farm boy, a widow, a grandfather. Your idea of what dire event Yeats is predicting in "The Second Coming" ("And what rough beast, its hour come round at last,/ Slouches towards Bethlehem to be born?") will depend on your religion, personality, and life experience. But that poem is clear enough!

6) *A good poem fulfills its promises.* What it sets out to do—musically, visually, emotionally—it accomplishes. At the end, the readers feel they have arrived. Consider these last lines: "A poem should not mean / but be" (Archibald MacLeish); "And Richard Cory, one calm summer night, / Went home and put a bullet through his head" (Edward Arlington Robinson); "Without a tighter

breathing / And Zero at the Bone—" (Emily Dickinson); "And the heaviest nuns walk in a pure floating / Of dark habits, / keeping their difficult balance" (Richard Wilbur). These lines, whether formal or free, are surprising, but prepared for by what's gone before, clicking into place like the last piece of a puzzle. They seem in retrospect inevitable.

In some ways, these "definitions" are vague descriptions—but if you apply them to your own poems, they can become quite specific. In the end, of course, good poems resist definition and explication. Like the natural objects of this world, they are what they are.

In my short poem on the next page, I've tried to capture what it feels like to want and/or need to write poetry, and what elements are necessary for its creation. But it's also a love poem. It's the nature of poetry, and of the world, to be more than one thing at once.

I should perhaps add that in this book I'll be using a lot of my own poems as examples, not because I think they're better than other poets', but because I have them at hand and know the processes that went into their writing. A brief word about the idiosyncratic punctuation in my poetry—there's a longer discussion in Chapter 4: I wrote for a long time using "normal" punctuation, and that was fine, but as I found I was using less and less of it, I developed, as you will notice in my quoted poems, a kind of limited punctuation: no periods, commas, dashes, semicolons, double quote marks; using spaces (two for commas, three for periods) and colons for clarification. I wanted a "cleaner" look, where my sonnets and free verse would be connected, at least visually, on the page. I like the way it looks (though I'll admit that all editors and critics do not!), and am comfortable with this style. I feel that I can say what I want this way, which is the main consideration. After listening to the critics who dislike it,

I decided I disagree with them, and will write this way until something else occurs to me that seems better. So now, here's the poem:

The Shells of Bermuda

First the wind through the window   lifting
this room with breath   tugging the curtains   waking
the flowers   turning one by one slowly
the pages of old books   Then the sun
through the windows   glinting in corners
warming the tops of tables   The cicadas'
shrill vibrations the woodpecker's percussion
even the high whine of Mrs Rheinhold
as she scolds her children   *Pamela*!   *Paul*!
All necessary: but the window most of all

There are moments in every day
when a hunger seizes and the hands
tremble and a wall turns transparent
or a cup speaks   Suddenly
bright as the shells of Bermuda
the combs for your long hair blaze on the desk

(first published in 2 Plus 2)

In this poem, I've tried to make a simple description of our house vibrate with suggestion. The hunger to write is fanned by the wind (inspiration), the sun (knowledge), the flowers (nature), old books (tradition), daily life (Mrs. Reinhold). But the most important thing for a writer is to be open (the window) to these experiences. Of course, I didn't plan all this in advance, I was just trying to describe our house and the way light glanced off a set of combs, but it's there, or something like it is there.

Writing poetry, like all writing for publication, is a tough game. It puts you on the line to be judged over and over, by yourself as well as others. I remember James

Dickey quoting with approval someone who said, in effect, "You shouldn't dive into the unconscious unless you're armed to the teeth." It's easy—and usually self-serving—to be pessimistic about the state of reading and writing in America today. But instead, I want to offer you three positive thoughts about writing and the writing life.

The first is, take an attitude toward your own work that I will call a kind of *stubborn modesty*. By "stubborn modesty" I mean that on the one hand, all of us need to be open to suggestions, advice, criticism, to be modest about our work. We can all learn. When we stop learning, our writing will curl up and go dead. When someone tells us something about our writing, we should listen, we should think about it, and sometimes we should even follow the given (and not always welcome) advice.

This modesty should apply particularly in two ways: 1) toward those editors, critics, and judges with more experience than we have had; and 2) to the great writers of previous generations. I'm convinced that you can't be a good poet, much less an outstanding one, without reading deeply among the famous poets who came before us. They are your schools, your teachers, and your best examples—and besides, this will save you from reinventing the wheel. And when poets read a lot of good poetry, some of the techniques learned will eventually show up in their own writing. We are what we read.

One of the odd occurrences that all teachers of writing have experienced is meeting a young person or beginner who wants to be a poet, but who has no favorite poems and has scarcely read any at all. If you say T. S. Eliot's *Waste Land* bores you, or you don't like Hart Crane or Wallace Stevens, or think that Emily Dickinson and Robert Frost are dated (all opinions I've heard)—those are judgments you should make only after the most careful consideration. These noted poets have moved and entertained generations of readers, and you should think carefully about why this is so.

At the same time, you have to be stubborn. If, after you've listened and considered and read and studied, you remain unconvinced, you've got to stick to your own guns, against editors, reviewers, the public—even the great writers of the past. Reverence toward the classics is a good trait, as long as it's honestly felt: When Samuel Johnson read *Paradise Lost*, he praised its strengths, but added, "None ever wished it longer than it is."

Writers are naturally subversive: They're born rule-breakers. As soon as a rule is stated—that poems have to be unified, for example, or have related images, or be written in stanzas—someone will successfully break the rule. But you have to know what you're doing, and why. We have poems without real words ("O frabjous day! Callooh! Callay!") and even poems without letters, like "Nightsong of the Fish" by the German poet Christian Morgenstern, who used dashes and tilted parentheses to indicate "fish music."

Like most poets, I break even my *own* rules sometimes:

Miss Arbuckle

Miss Arbuckle taught seventh grade
She hid her lips against her teeth
Her bottom   like the ace of spades
was guarded by   the virgin queen

Miss Arbuckle wore thick-soled shoes
blue dresses with white polka dots
She followed and enforced the rules
What she was paid to teach   she taught

She said that Wordsworth liked the woods
that Blake had never seen a tiger

that Byron wasn't always good
but died in Greece   a freedom fighter

She gave her students rigid tests
and when the school let out in June
she painted rings around her breasts
and danced by the light of the moon

   (first published in *Educational Forum*)

(The rule here, of course, was that you can't use certain rhymes anymore, *especially* "June" and "moon"—
they've been taken over by Hallmark Cards; but as soon
as I said this out loud I was itching to rhyme them, which
involved yanking them out of the normal romantic context and using them in a semester context.)

   The second point I want to make, though not new, is
You have to be tough. Hemingway, who published a book
of poems when he was young, said, I've been told, in his
rare French, *Il faut durer.* You've got to endure, collect
rejections, lose contests. (Hemingway as you know lost
an entire manuscript, his first novel, but he got back to
his desk and wrote *The Sun Also Rises.*) And in order to
endure, you have to like the actual process of writing and
rewriting.

   Writing is worth doing, whether you publish it or not.
I think Emily Dickinson was happiest when she was
writing, her poems piling up like old love letters in her
closet; she listened politely to, and decided to ignore, her
more experienced critics. If you're hooked on the physical
act of writing, you have a good chance of staying at it long
enough to say what you were born to say. And if someone
recognizes and rewards this, that's a bonus.

   My third point is more interesting, I think, because it
hasn't been done enough. Poets should *be more generous
with one another.* Writing is such a lonely activity that
we need all the help we can get, but in actual practice,

poets are often destructively competitive. Americans in particular have practiced what I call the "macho theory of literature": Writing has become a sport like football or boxing. Reviewers root through a book of poems like a barrel of apples, tossing the good ones away, looking for the one with a worm.

Many of you have read in some detail about the lives of poets in preceding generations: Allen Tate, Hart Crane, Theodore Roethke, Elizabeth Bishop, Delmore Schwartz, Randall Jarrell, John Berryman, Robert Lowell, Sylvia Plath, and many others. They attacked writers whom they considered rivals and enemies with merciless hostility, and toward the end of their lives they attacked each other. It was an unhealthy atmosphere, and the personal lives of many of these brilliant people were disastrous—and I believe it hurt their writing, too.

One of my hopes is that the current influx of women into the ranks of writers will help create the network of support that has long been needed, a lack that writing workshops have partly filled. Women writers, in my experience, seem more skilled at cooperation than their male counterparts, who are still playing King of the Hill. (I'm aware, of course, of Kipling's observation that "the female of the species is more deadly than the male," but I hope this applies mainly to "she-bears," as in his poem.) Finally, of course, poets are not female or male or black or Southern or Chicano or Jewish or young or old: We're writers, working together whether we want to or not.

Right now writers are in a transitional period, a difficult time as our literature is getting reassessed and shaken up; everybody's a little nervous and edgy, but I'm hopeful that as time goes on we will be a more cooperative group, where the idea will be for each person to write as well as he or she can. History will sort out who is "major" or "minor."

Specifically, give your fellow poets more time, more slack, more help. Everyone needs help. Share information, buy them a drink. Encourage them. Everyone needs encouragement. Obviously, strict criticism—tough love—is needed as well, but in poetry, as in life, this works only in an atmosphere of trust and support.

These three suggestions, then: Cultivate a stubborn modesty; stay in for the long run; and be generous with your fellow writers. Perhaps we can't help ourselves and will do what we do no matter what anyone says or doesn't say. I'll sum up this thought with a poem I wrote for our daughter, an artist living in Italy. The words for her apply equally well to you:

To A Daughter With Artistic Talent

I know why   getting up in the cold dawn
you paint cold yellow houses
and silver trees   Look at those green birds
almost real   and that lonely child looking
at   those houses and trees
You paint (the best way) without reasoning
to see what you feel   and green birds
are what a child sees

Some gifts are not given: you
are delivered to them
bound by chains of nerves and genes
stronger than iron or steel   although
unseen   You have painted every day
for as long as I can remember
and will be painting still
when you read this   some cold
and distant December when the child
is old and the trees no longer silver
but black fingers scratching a gray sky

And you never know why (I was lying
before when I said I knew)

You never know the force that drives you wild
to paint that sky   those birds flying
and is never satisfied today
but maybe tomorrow
when the sky is a surreal sea
in which you drown . . .

I tell you this with love and pride
and sorrow   my artist child
while the birds change from green to blue to brown . . .

(first published in *Motive*)

℘. 2

The Sources of Poetry

THE PAINTER Henri Matisse said, "To work is to live without dying!" And the simplest answer to the question, "Where do poems come from?" is "*hard work.*" I'm skeptical of inspiration. Although it's part of the creative process, *waiting* for inspiration is too often an excuse to avoid writing.

We almost always begin writing poems in imitation of other poems that we've read and admired; for early starters, nursery rhymes, A. A. Milne, and Robert Louis Stevenson are marvelous models. I can remember running around our house in Brooklyn chanting, "Alice is marrying one of the guard. / 'A soldier's life is terrible hard,' / Says Alice." I liked the fact that Milne used "terrible" instead of "terribly"—an early example of the freedom poets have.

When we read something we admire, we feel moved and want to write to recreate the experience: Writing is an act of homage. In high school I tried to write like Edgar Allan Poe; in college I imitated John Donne. Allen Ginsberg's first book was rhymed verse similar to William Blake's; Howard Nemerov's first collection sounded very much like William Butler Yeats; T. S. Eliot's early poems were modeled on the French symbolists; W. S.

Merwin, whose father was a Presbyterian minister, began by writing hymns. Nikki Giovanni was influenced by Robert Louis Stevenson, Seamus Heaney by Gerard Manley Hopkins. Marianne Moore claimed that everything she wrote was the result of reading someone else.

It doesn't matter at all where you begin. These early imitations are good exercises. What does matter is that in time you discover your own voice.

We begin with other poets because that's where we learn about poetry, but what do we write about? And what's the primary source of our desire to write? Although this is complicated to analyze, I think that art must come (in part) from some powerful emptiness or lack, even though it's sometimes hard to know exactly what's missing.

While there must always be some exception somewhere, I believe the perfectly happy person would not write poetry (or fiction or compose music or make art, etc.) The critic Judith Kitchen has said that "the poet's natural empathy stems from experienced pain." And in "The Solace of Poems," Susan Ludvigson writes, "To discover them/ is to link with the unbroken/griefs we name and rename." Poetry is a way of making our problems bearable.

At the same time, the suffering poet is an irritating cliche. The idea of the poet as extra-sensitive has become laughable, despite the fact that some poets really are— but so are some accountants, dockworkers, fishmongers. After all, Wallace Stevens and Archibald MacLeish were lawyers, Dana Gioia's a businessman, Ted Kooser an insurance executive, Ann Darr a pilot. James Dickey was a successful advertising man for Coca-Cola. What differentiates poets from others is that they're able to *articulate* whatever sensitivity they have.

While some poets (Robert Lowell, Sylvia Plath, John

Berryman, Anne Sexton) have or had publicly tempestu-
ous lives, many others do not (William Stafford, Richard
Wilbur, Josephine Jacobsen, William Meredith). It's not
necessary to suffer publicly, or even in a garret, to be a
poet. A poet's job isn't to suffer, but to bear witness. Suffering will come whether you want it to or not; it's not
that special. Here's a sonnet of mine, more or less on the
subject:

Short Meditation on Long-Suffering Poets

Although they tell us suffering helps one write
tears have nothing to do with making poems:
I know a man who rocks and moans all night
and every line he cries lies dry as bone
Teardrop   and *blood-drop*   are only words
and though one write like Faust in reddest ink
unsealing veins of salt that bite and burn
it's vowels and consonants   not blood   we drink

The nightingale's a feather of a bird:
nature's breath can knock it head to tail
A poet should be tougher   Some have heard
the mockingbird scaling like a nightingale
I know a woman   hasn't wept for years:
and every syllable she writes sheds tears

(first published in *Tar River Poetry*)

Perhaps a poet's need to write is like the oyster's irri-
tation from the grain of sand. Something is bothering him
or her, and the result, with luck, is a pearl: Although
these may be of greatly differing value, they're all pearls!

I think our first poems come unbidden, from loneliness or love, or both; from something deep within us that
needs special expression. But some beginning writers
bring—if not at first, then later—something extra: a love
of language and the clarity it can convey. These are the

writers who become poets. "Life wounds everyone. Besides blood, however, the artist also sheds light" (Alfred Corn).

As we continue to write poems and come to recognize or feel a calling, we discover a need to organize our efforts so we'll be able to do our best, keep the source open, say everything we want to say. The methods will differ from person to person, but many "devices" are time-tested and open to us. For me, the five main ones are: 1) Write on a regular schedule; 2) Read as much as you can; 3) Keep a notebook or journal; 4) Tap into your dreams; and 5) Stay close to the other arts, especially painting and music. The last of these is closest to the source of poetry.

Five miles from the college where I taught for twenty-seven years, is the Salvador Dali Museum. Early on in each course, I would try to bring the students there for an afternoon. I made no assignment, no attempt to get them to write a poem about a particular painting, and yet Dali crept (or "melted") into the poems of a large percentage of the students, as well as into some of mine:

O Switzerland where is your Dada now?
Where is your boomboomboom your
rosy Anna Blossom?
In the closet Dada's in the closet
where your little triggers fatten
like commas around a stiff proposition
where Freud forever sucks Napoleon's fingers
and there the lederhosen grin like clamshells
there the albino dwarf chewing on chickenbones . . .

(from "Lines from Neuchâtel,"
first published by Konglomerati Press)

Painting and poetry have been twinned since antiquity. "As is painting, so is poetry," wrote the Latin poet Horace in his *Ars Poetica*. "Painters and poets alike have always had license to dare anything." For centuries artists have used literature and poetry for their inspiration: the Bible stories, Ovid's "Metamorphoses," the legends about Venus, and Shakespeare's Ophelia spring to mind. Two of our greatest modern artists, Francis Bacon and David Hockney, acknowledge their debts to T. S. Eliot and Wallace Stevens, respectively. The influence doesn't have to be direct to be important. Tone, attitude, and approach can be more influential than subject matter.

And, particularly in the nineteenth and twentieth centuries, poets have used paintings and sculpture, and, to a lesser extent, music as sources of their inspiration. We should all, be familiar with poems such as W. H. Auden's "Musee des Beaux Arts" (on Brueghel's "Fall of Icarus"), Rainer Maria Rilke's "Archaic Torso of Apollo," and William Butler Yeats's "Leda and the Swan." These are on everyone's list of great poems. For those of you inclined to pursue this connection, here's a selected and random list of poems centering around art or music.

Poems on Art

Abse, Dannie: "At the Tate" (Rodin)
Ashbery, John: "Self-Portrait in a Convex Mirror" (Parmigianino)
Adams, Anna: "Totes Meer" (Paul Nash)
Auden, W. H.: "Musee des Beaux Arts" (Brueghel)
Bishop, Elizabeth: "The Monument"
Bly, Robert: "A Chunk of Amethyst"
Chappell, Fred: "Voyagers" (Vermeer)
Clampitt, Amy: "Archaic Figure" (sculpture)
Corn, Alfred: "Chinese Porcelains at the Metropolitan"
Dobyns, Stephen: "The Street" (Balthus)
Ferlinghetti, Lawrence: "Short Story on a Painting by Gustav Klimt"
Hacker, Marilyn: "La Fontaine de Vaucluse" (Jean Antoine)
Hall, Jim: "The Whittler"

Hardy, Thomas: "Christmas in the Elgin Room" (Elgin marbles)

Hirsch, Edward: "Edward Hopper and the House by the Railroad"

Hughes, Ted: "To Paint a Water Lily" (Monet)

Jarrell, Randall: "The Bronze David of Donatello"

Kennedy, X. J. : "Nude Descending Staircase" (Duchamp)

Kumin, Maxine: "The Bridge-Builder" (Charles Ellet, Jr.)

Levertov, Denise: "Winter Afternoon in the V & A"

Lowell, Robert: "For the Union Dead" (St. Gaudens)

Ludvigson, Susan: "The Artist"

Martınez, Dionisio: "Matisse: Blue Nude"

McClatchy, J. D.: "A Capriccio of Roman Ruins and Sculpture"

Meinke, Peter: "The Azure Falcon" (Leonardo Lasansky)

Meredith, William: *Hazard, the Painter*

Merwin, W. S.: "Two Paintings by Alfred Wallis"

Mueller, Lisel: "Paul Delvaux: The Village of the Mermaids"

Nemerov, Howard: "The Painter Dreaming in the Scholar's House" (Klee)

Nims, John Frederick: "Fuori Stagione"

O'Hara, Frank: "On Seeing Larry Rivers' 'Crossing the Delaware' "

Ostriker, Alicia: "At the Van Gogh Museum"

Pastan, Linda: "Fresco" (Massaccio)

Piercy, Marge: "A Work of Artifice" (bonsai)

Plath, Sylvia: "Death & Co." (Leonard Baskin's woodcut of Blake)

Pound, Ezra: "Of Jacopo Del Sellaio"

Rich, Adrienne: "Aunt Jennifer's Tigers" (quilting)

Rilke, Rainer Maria: "Archaic Torso of Apollo"

Schwartz, Delmore: "Seurat's Sunday Afternoon Along the Seine"

Sexton, Anne: "The Starry Night" (Van Gogh)

Smith, Stevie: "Spanish School"

Song, Cathy: "Girl Powdering Her Neck" (Utamaro)

Stevens, Wallace: "The Man With the Blue Guitar" (Picasso)

Tate, James: "Read the Great Poets"

Wallace, Robert: "Giacometti's Dog"

Wilbur, Richard: "Museum Piece" (Degas)

Williams, W. C.: *Pictures from Brueghel*

Wright, Charles: "Portrait of the Poet in Abraham Von Werdt's
Dream"
Yeats, W. B.: "Leda and the Swan"

Poems on Music

Auden, W. H.: "The Duet"
Bly, Robert: "Ocean Rain and Music"
Chappell, Fred: "The Gift to be Simple" (Copland)
Clampitt, Amy: "Dancers Exercising"
Curbelo, Silvia: "Janis Joplin"
Jarrell, Randall: "The Player Piano"
Justice, Donald: "The Pupil" (piano lessons)
Kumin, Maxine: "Rehearsing for the Final Reckoning"
(Berlioz)
Livesay, Dorothy: "Bartok and the Geranium"
Martınez, Dionisio: "Afternoons with Satie"
Meinke, Peter: "Minuet in G" (Beethoven)
Nemerov, Howard: "Playing the Inventions" (Bach)
O'Brien, Laurie: "Sonata Facile" (Mozart)
O'Hara, Frank: "On Rachmaninoff's Birthday"
Oliver, Mary: "Robert Schumann"
Ostriker, Alicia: "The Eighth and the Thirteenth"
(Shostakovich)
Zimmer, Paul: "The Duke Ellington Dream"

These poems will give you some idea how important
the arts can be as a source for poetry. It's not a matter of
simply seeing, say, a great engraving like Durer's "The
Knight, Death, and the Devil," and writing a poem about
it, though that can happen. (Randall Jarrell did it.) Usually, as with your first impulse to write poetry as an act
of homage to another poet, a writer may be moved by the
creativity of the artist or composer, by the contagious energy that flows through a particular painting or symphony. A writer's natural impulse is to translate this
energy into words, as an artist translates it into paint or
a musician into notes.

Sometimes, too, the source of poetry has to do with

the setting—the room, house, concert hall or museum—or the juxtaposition of one work of art with another. Some years ago, when I read that color is a
"property of light that depends on wave length," I wondered if that meant that works of art are colorless at
night, when the museum closes its doors. I could see
these masterpieces relaxing in the evening, slipping off
their colors—letting their hair down, as it were—and it
led me to a vision of the paintings as villagers gossiping
when the sun goes down:

Talk of the Paintings

At night the paintings roll up their colors
like ribbons and slide from their frames
pale as 'Casablanca' ˏ visiting in the dark
Mon Dieu   shouts Dejeuner
are the women getting skinny or what?
Ach   mein freund   says Bathsheba
they are not loved   I hear them   there
is no time: business   always business

Monkey business   if you ask me   says Mona Lisa
laughing out loud   *Ciao   amica*

O the paintings gossip by the fountain
a convention of flower-loving nudists
of rich merchants and warriors
their vowels and consonants mounting
in a babel of pure sound
meaning absolutely nothing
The museum is relaxed   happy:
and then the doors open

The paintings hear your footsteps   They tense
You turn and they explode in light
                    (first published in *Yankee*)

In this poem I wanted to convey the energy of art
("They explode in light") and also its playfulness. Though

life is a serious experience that ends badly, a great deal of it is playful, and this is reflected in poetry and the arts in general. While many notable exceptions can be found, a book of poems that elicits no smiles at all is a long book indeed, and usually not true to life as we experience it. A wonderful way to get the feel for the variety and exuberance of life is to go to museums and galleries and concerts and recitals. These have been and will continue to be unending sources of poetry for all of us.

When I thought of the idea for "Talk of the Paintings," I jotted it down in the little notebook I always carry. I wrote "Color is a property of light, so when the lights are out there's no color." Then later, at a museum, I added "At night paintings roll up their colors and slide from their frames pale as *Casablanca*"—more or less the first line of the poem. I had probably seen the Bogart film recently (still in black and white), but this I don't remember.

Notebooks can be a rich resource for poets, as is evident in the published notebooks of Anton Chekhov, Theodore Roethke, Louise Bogan, and May Sarton, but more often they're just useful tools in the background, priceless in helping us remember fleeting thoughts that we can work on and delve into and expand later. Wordsworth's definition of poetry helps us here. "Poetry is the spontaneous overflow of powerful feelings: it takes its origin from emotion recollected in tranquillity." (Wordsworth, remember, was famous, or infamous, for using his sister Dorothy's notebooks for inspiration.) Notebooks help us hold onto those spontaneous thoughts and visions that, by definition, can't be controlled and come to us at odd moments, at parties, or when driving or jogging or dreaming.

I've never been disciplined enough to keep a regular journal, though I've had long streaks when I'd write something in my notebook just about every day. I like to write in it, and I like carrying it around. (I have a small black leather-covered notebook that fits in my pocket.) A journal is for meditation and summation—an excellent practice if you can find or create the time; a notebook is for random jottings, quick thoughts—which are often your best, or strangest, thoughts.

Heather McHugh is accurate, I think, when she says there's something erotic about a notebook: secret, private, personal, intense. *The Poet's Notebook*, edited by Stephen Kuusisto, Deborah Tall, and David Weiss, is an excellent collection of excerpts from the notebooks of contemporary American poets. In it, Mary Oliver writes that a good notebook entry should be "Something totally unexpected, like a barking cat." All of us have moments in a day when we think like no one else. A notebook or a journal preserves those thoughts so they can be used later in poems. *The Writer's Journal: 40 Contemporary Writers and their Journals*, edited by Sheila Binder, is another exemplary and useful collection.

I suppose we're most original in our dreams, being in our freest and most uncensored state. I often have difficulty recalling mine, but have trained myself to be better at it than I used to be, and to try to write them down in my notebook as soon as I wake up. Dreams offer good material for poems *because* they're irrational and multileveled, with a strange and hallucinatory clarity. They sometimes *seem* to have some hidden meaning—and often do, as Freud has shown. Poems should probe for meaning under life's surface, and dreams are a good place to begin.

Poet David Baker believes that "the poet's purpose is to establish, represent, and articulate mystery," and dreams are mysteries available to us all. Sometimes just an image remains; sometimes larger sequences can be saved. I played baseball in high school, and a few years back began having a repeated dream of missing a ball because it was thrown at me so hard. Here's the beginning of the poem that resulted:

A Dream of Third Base

Night after night   frozen at third base
I lean toward a throw I know I must catch
but don't stretch far enough:
the ball sails off   the runner
slides snarling at my feet   Then
right away and once again
bare-handed as before the fall
perched on third in the starless air
the runner's shadow darkening the path
I wait for the accursed ball

I think I'm afraid it will hurt:
the ball is coming too fast
The catcher with his thick wrists
has reared and fired like a loaded gun:
or the snake-eyed shortstop whose lidless eyes . . .

Surely baseball stands for something else
I haven't been a fan
since the Dodgers abandoned Ebbett's Field
We used to go on Sundays   my dad and I
breaking the Fourth Commandment . . .

The field is Paradise   then   all green and new:
we're young and quick of foot   our cries
rise in the springtime air

And then we're given a ball
And then we're given a bat
Who are those men in black?

It starts hurting after that . . .

The poem goes on, trying to make sense of all of this, by quoting Dante's dreamlike *Inferno*, among other things. Most of the details accumulated in my notebook as the dream kept recurring, and my job as a poet was to piece them together in a way that would recreate the emotion the dream aroused in me. At any rate, dreams are invaluable to poets: Use them the way archaeologists use dinosaur bones or shards of pottery. (I first typed "shards of *poetry*"!)

Although not necessary, keeping a regular schedule is also helpful to most poets. When I was younger, I wrote at night, often after midnight when our four children were asleep. This might explain why my first book was called *The Night Train and the Golden Bird*. Now that I tend to get sleepy around ten p.m., I prefer writing in the morning—which, in an informal and totally unreliable survey, I found that most other writers do as well, working out some kind of balance between their writing lives and their communal lives.

I believe, by the way, that poets *do* have responsibilities beyond their art: to their families, friends, communities, countries. This must vary from person to person, but someone whose life is *all* art seems to me unconnected, precious, and hollow.

I like to write approximately from 8:00 a.m. to noon, but many poets get up much earlier, in order to get their writing in before the regular working day begins. William Stafford was famous for getting up early, in the dark, every day of his life, no matter where he was, and writing at least one poem. I think it's more important to write regularly than to write a lot at a time. If you write a little every day, at the end of the year you'll have a manuscript.

So, to summarize: The sources for poetry are deep

within yourself, and they can be brought to the surface with the help of the methods discussed here. "Seek the depth of things," advised Rilke in his extraordinary *Letters to a Young Poet*. "*Everything* is gestation and then bringing forth."

𝕰. 3

Poems and Meaning

I T'S MARVELOUS to read Boswell's *Life of Johnson*.
Johnson offers poets the lesson that though he was
often wrong, he always strove to make his observations
exact, well phrased, and pithy, including this familiar ex-
change on the topic under discussion:

> "Sir, what is poetry?"
> "Why Sir, it is much easier to say what it is not. We
> all *know* what light is; but it is not easy to *tell* what it
> is."

So Samuel Johnson is my excuse for starting this
chapter on "meaning" with a negative: Poems don't have
to mean anything.

A frequent mistake of many poets is Having Something to Say. This is not because saying something is
wrong, but because it tends to distract from the main ob-
jective: saying something *memorably*, beautifully. Permanently. "Poetry is news that *stays news*" (Ezra Pound).
And what makes it stay news is how it's said, not what it
says. I believe we do write poetry to communicate—for
example, Emily Dickinson's "This is my letter to the
World/That never wrote to Me"—but the key point here

is that a good poem is not *just* communication. A poem needs to be a delicate *balance* of music and communication.

Think of your favorite poems. "Stopping By Woods On A Snowy Evening"? Lovely description of an all-too-familiar scene, clear as a glass of water. Or is it? Is it really about death, or even suicide? Well, maybe. It's often what's *not* said that makes poems memorable. Novelists are putters-in, poets are leavers-out.

"The Love Song of J. Alfred Prufrock"? We have lots of studies of indecisive men. What makes this one unforgettable? Is it about T. S. Eliot's sex life? Is it about an entire repressed society? It doesn't matter, does it? Lines like "I have heard the mermaids singing, each to each" will haunt you your entire life.

"O, my Luve's like a red red rose," wrote Robert Burns. This may or may not have been true, but who cares? Or more to the point, "As silent as a mirror is believed / Realities plunge in silence by . . ." is the beginning of Hart Crane's poem, "Legend." I'm not sure what it means (it *seems* to mean something), but I've always loved it. You will have your own examples.

Poets position themselves along a continuum of meaning. On one side Edward Field writes straightforward lines like "My mother's family was made up of loving women," and on the other John Ashbery writes "the unplanted cabbages stand tearful out of the mist." The Ashbery school (in critical ascendance today) takes the position that meaning is boring and bourgeois. Straight information is too easy. "Surprise us—tell us something we don't know!" is their cry. The Field side takes the common-sense point of view that poetry belongs to the people, and if it doesn't make sense, who wants it? Surreal gibberish is also easy: "The feathered lamp drinks with shifty eyes."

Both sides reflect a Puritan ethic that both sides deny. *What we do is hard work*, each says, and they're both right. (But it's no use telling your friends how hard you work as a poet: They won't believe it. Better to go along with the wit who said, "The trouble with being a poet is what to do with the other twenty-three hours." That will make your friends jealous.)

Of course, I'm exaggerating, but the point is that *you can station yourself anywhere along the meaning continuum, and you will still be "right."* For the sake of your poetry, let the words, the sounds, the rhythms, the images come first, and let the meaning follow. Even Carl Sandburg, one of our most direct poets, said, "What can be explained is not poetry"—meaning, I'm sure, it's the music of the words that's important. To put it in a spiritual or religious context, where I believe poetry ultimately belongs, "The way that can be spoken of is not the True Way" (Lao-tze, founder of Taoism).

And yet . . . and yet we want poems to *mean something*, and many of them do, but with this startling complication: *They mean different things to different people, and even different things to the same person at different times.* Those are the best poems.

Anyone who has done a lot of editing for magazines, or judging for contests, will testify to the mind-numbing experience of reading piles of indecipherable poetry. Howard Nemerov, after wading for hours through manuscripts, most of which apparently followed MacLeish's dictum, "A poem should not mean, / But be," once said, "Well, there they all were, and they didn't mean anything."

The American composer Charles Ives said, "You cannot set art off in a corner and hope for it to have vitality, reality, and substance." I think the best poems come *out* of that corner, *tending* toward meaning, leaving space for us to move around but at the same time giving us hints, pushing us in a general direction. This doesn't mean that a poem can mean *anything*: "Stopping by Woods," for example, isn't about communism (as a student of mine once claimed). There are no directional hints leading us that way.

To try to trace the development of meaning in a poem, I've chosen semi-randomly one of mine called "Apples," because it's short, I remember how I wrote it, and it refers to Samuel Johnson:

Apples

The apple I see and the apple
I think I see and the apple
I say I see
are at least three
different apples . . .
One sympathizes with Dr. Johnson here
when he kicked a stone
to dispute the Bishop: such
airy-fairy distinctions   So much
applesauce!

And yet when you say
what I think you say
in a way that may
or may not be final I can only hope
that cold stone   that white boulder   that . . .
iceberg between us
is not really there but is sliding
like some titanic idea
through the North Pole
in the apple of my eye

(first published in *Poetry*)

What does the poem mean? I wrote it, and I'm not entirely sure! Stanley Kunitz has said that a "poem does not tell what it means, even to its maker." And Hayden Carruth wrote that "no poet can say what his or her poems are about, because no poet can *see* what his or her poems are about." But we can make educated guesses.

"Apples" seems to be a love poem that takes its time getting about its business. Perhaps—translated into prose—it could go like this: Two lovers have had an argument, and one of them is hoping that this coldness on his or her part isn't permanent, but is just passing through. That's it. Not very interesting, unless you identify with the lovers (which readers of course sometimes do).

What's interesting are the apples.

The poem began, as most of mine do, with a phrase or sentence. I had been talking with a friend about memory, and more or less the first sentence "came out": "The apple I see, the apple I think I see, and the apple I *say* I see are at least three different apples." So I wrote it down in my notebook. This I suppose is the "inspiration" part of composition. (I visualize the composition of a poem as a series of little explosions, like Chinese firecrackers, each one setting off the next.)

What intrigued me about the sentence was the repetition of "apple" four times and "see" three times. When, later, I moved the lines around to emphasize the repetition, I also saw the rhyme of "see" and "three," so I wrote "I say I see" as a separate line, using the sound and look of it as part of a five-line stanza (the end-words being "apple / apple / see / three / apples"—a nice little poem by itself.

While doing this (everything happens simultaneously in poetry, which is one of the exciting things about writing it), I remembered from Boswell's biography the famous rebuttal on this general subject that Dr. Johnson made to the Idealist philosopher, Bishop Berkeley. Berkeley had theorized that matter, the real world, was non-existent, that it's all in our heads—and Johnson and Boswell were having a tough time logically refuting him, until Johnson "struck his foot against a large stone," saying "I refute it *thus*." And thus that old rascal Samuel Johnson entered this poem about apples.

His entrance was a change in direction, so I indented it, and as I tinkered with the poem, or the *possible* poem, I could see that "stone" went well with "Johnson" and "distinctions," and that led me to our slang word for too much fancy talk or overly sophisticated reasoning (which is what Johnson was accusing Berkeley of): "applesauce." *Voila!* We're brought back to the original image of apples, but this time also thinking about language and the strange way it works. Robert Frost said that the art of poetry involves "the taking advantage of happy accidents."

One question that the "Johnson section" of the poem brings up is how much knowledge to expect from a reader. The answer today seems to be, as our canon of required reading shifts, changes, and dwindles—not much. Our task as writers, however, is *not* to avoid using learned or private references, but to use them clearly and/or to good effect. The reference to Samuel Johnson and Bishop Berkeley will be familiar to most college-educated readers, but those who have never heard of these eighteenth-century gentlemen won't have trouble following the poem. They'll miss only the little pleasure one gets from recognizing an apt illustration, and after all, if they're interested enough, they can look it up.

In "The Love Song of J. Alfred Prufrock," T. S. Eliot writes:

> There will be time to murder and create,
> And time for all the works and days of hands
> That lift and drop a question on your plate . . .

It's a wonderful sentence, and if you recognize the
ironic reference to *Works and Days* by the eighth-century
farmer-philosopher Hesiod, so much the better, but it's
hardly necessary for your enjoyment of the lines.

As I wrote "Apples," despite some rhyme, it seemed
destined to be in free verse: No set form was emerging.
But I saw I could make a kind of loose pattern by making
the Dr. Johnson section also five lines, to match the open-
ing sentence; and then to reinforce it by end-rhyming
"such" and "much"—words that wouldn't be emphasized
in a straight sentence—to match "see" and "free" in the
first section. The reader won't care about this sort of
thing, but it's very important that the poet care, trying
his or her best to line up "the best words in the best
order."

Now I had ten lines, a beginning of sorts, but where
was I going? *What did it mean?* Frost said a poem, like a
chunk of ice, has to glide on its own melting, and as I sat
thinking of the lines I had written—though mostly about
apples—I suddenly understood it was going to be a love
poem. Why? I'm not sure, but I think "apple" suggested
"Eve" and the apple of knowledge, the apple of tempta-
tion. And, even closer to this poem, as it turned out,
there's the golden apple, the Apple of Discord inscribed
"to the fairest" and thrown out by Eris to make trouble
among the beautiful goddesses. We also have love-apples
(tomatoes) and apple-blossom time. There are so many
different apples!

I didn't reason all this out, but most poems, even little
poems like this one, move toward meaning in associative
ways. Gabriele Rico, in *Writing the Natural Way*, calls
this method "clustering." Pick the central image from
your poem and fill your page (or your head) with associ-
ated and uncensored related words, images, and ideas—

then use the ones that help the poem by being closest to the sound and meaning you're striving for.

Because I was also thinking about language, I began to write about how we talk to one another, how easy it is to misunderstand. I had to match those apples verbally (words, like apples, also vary in context, depending on whether you're saying, hearing, or remembering them—as any trial lawyer can point out). I tried to reproduce the loose rhyme of the first stanza with the "say / say," "may / may" repetitions. I wanted to bring Dr. Johnson's stone back as a kind of metaphor for a lover's spat. That led to the final "idea" of the poem.

The "o" sound of "stone" went well with "hope." To emphasize it, because it fit emotionally, I made it "cold stone," then "white boulder." The natural next mental step from cold stone and white boulder was to think of a glacier or an iceberg. And the iceberg led me, as it would many Americans, to remember the sinking of the "unsinkable ship," the *Titanic*, in 1912.

So the ingredients were all gathered. I hadn't known it when I began, but by this time I knew I was writing a love poem using apples and icebergs as metaphors for the difficulties of communication. A metaphor doesn't *explain* anything; rather, it creates a new situation that is in some ways the emotional and intellectual equivalent of the original feeling or thought. I think a major appeal of poetry is that this feeling is orchestrated by the power of language to organize what is essentially disorganized experience, a temporary balancing act. *Let the language guide you, and the meaning will follow.* If you reverse that emphasis, you're heading toward propaganda and advertisement, and away from the natural music of the language.

What was left for me to do in this poem was to tie the two images—apples and icebergs—together in some satisfying way. Is this always necessary? I doubt it, but I tend to work that way, the way a musical composition often fuses themes at the end. And language came to my rescue, as it will do if you're patient. The phrase, "apple of my eye," usually means "my true love, my favorite"; so the most obvious reading of the poem is that the speaker hopes this misunderstanding is not permanent but is passing through some cold part (the North Pole) of his lover's mind, and will soon be gone.

It can also mean, however, that this idea is only in the poet's mind; it's something that he's seeing that may or may not be there. Like Heisenberg's uncertainty principle, it depends where you're standing.

In addition, the word "titanic" shadows the poem considerably. It means (the denotation) "enormous," like the ancient Gods, the Titans. But in this context, we'll certainly think of the doomed ship (the connotation). So what began as a lighthearted poem ends ambiguously on a darkening image.

The progression of love from delight to disaster is a tale that has been written thousands and thousands of times. This poem mirrors that lifelike situation and recreates it. I don't think the meaning of the poem is very difficult; it's like life, a little slippery to get hold of. (What's the meaning of *your* life, or mine?) And yet linguistically "Apples" comes together—I hope—to give the reader a sense of closure missing from real-life experiences.

I randomly chose this poem to illustrate the relation of meaning to poetry, but I now see it's *about* meaning, so it may not have been as random as I thought (I sometimes think *nothing* is random). Mainly I wanted to say, trust the language. If it wants to mean something to you, it will.

This is easy to say but hard to do. We all have ideas,

often very praiseworthy ones, that we want to inflict on other people: Love one another, take care of the trees, don't be a pig, etc. But my experience leads me to believe that your ideas are going to come through in spite of yourself, no matter what you do. Any book will make this clear. If you read a collection of even the most impenetrable poems, by the time you come to the end, you pretty much know what the author thinks on a great many subjects.

Instead of worrying about meaning, worry about whether you've used too many adverbs, or what word you should end your line on (should it be a preposition?). Of course you should feel passionately about your poems. Blood and tears should spill on the page, but if you need to be *told* to be passionate, you're in the wrong line of work.

Worry also about the connotations of your words, and their sounds. Especially their sounds. People—friends, classmates, teachers, reviewers—will disagree as to which words go best where. This makes things difficult, but it's what poets do. Marianne Moore said, "There is no easy way if you are to be a great artist; and the nature of one, in achieving his art, is different from the nature of another."

On the "meaning continuum," I'm on the side that favors a high degree of clarity. An entry in James Dickey's journal is: "Blazing clearness. The blazing clearness. How to get it?" Even a critic like Christian Wiman, who seems to prefer "difficult" poetry, has written in *Poetry* Magazine, "The real difficulty is in being clear. . .without sacrificing depth or complexity."

Handling the language, with all its wonderful tricks and surprises, to the best of your ability—that's what's important. Wallace Stevens said that we read poetry with our nerves; as writers we need to reach past our rational minds and make our poems visceral. In a world where everything seems unrelated, chaotic, and fragmented, the language of poetry has this great innate ability to embody the interconnectedness of things: "O, my Luve's like a red red rose." Absolutely.

The novelist F. Scott Fitzgerald, who also published poetry in *The New Yorker*, said that the mark of an intelligent mind is to be capable of holding two opposed ideas at the same time, and still retain the ability to function. Poetry has ideas, but not necessarily *rational* ideas. Fitzgerald had probably read the letters of John Keats (which every poet should do) and was remembering Keats's delightful sentence, "What shocks the virtuous philosopher, delights the camelion poet."

Americans are impatient with poetry for this very reason. A common cry is, "Why don't they say what they mean?" And it's true, for various historical reasons, that poetry (Eliot, Pound, Stevens, Crane) became more "difficult" in the twentieth century, as did art and music (Picasso, Braque, Schonberg, Stravinsky). Artists, pushed by photography, became more interested in the texture of paint than in their subjects; and poets, pushed by the novel, became more interested in the sound of their words than in their meaning. What was once a window became more like a mirror.

Because poetry involves depth, because it's the kind of writing in which *everything* matters—spacing, sound, punctuation, word order, secondary meanings—it's slow going; and everything in our culture works against this. We eat fast, we walk fast, we work fast, and we like to read fast. (Television, which presents short interrupted scenes, is the perfect medium for this hopped-up contemporary pace.)

Poetry wants to put on the brakes, to puzzle us a little, make us use our imaginations. For many people this isn't easy. But the difficulties of poetry should be like the difficulties of life: not academic, but mysterious. I mentioned "impenetrable poetry" earlier. Here's one of my dream-influenced poems that begins with that idea:

Teacups

Life is
Life is impenetrable
'And this   my dear   is the kitchen'
'Forgive me   my dear   I *believe* this is the bedroom'
'Well yes   you may be right . . .'
And trees
trees used to have acorns
but now teacups fall gently from their branches
Yards fill with broken porcelain
'Delightful tea, my dear'
'I'm sorry   *cherie*   but this is bourbon'
'Ah yes   I should have known . . .'
Children are everywhere
in the kitchen   under the trees
the cries of children overpower our lives
'Mommy!   Daddy!'
'Yes children   Yes my dears?'
'Kiss off   old folks
Rake up those goddam teacups'

(first published in *Trying to Surprise God*)

Rather than meaning anything in particular, this poem is like a painting or a little surrealist play. J. D. McClatchy has said that poems tend to "emerge" before we sit down to "work them up." This one emerged from a dream, which is about all I can say about it. In this dream that I mostly forgot, I remembered the trees had teacups instead of leaves, and so I began writing, beginning with the middle lines: "trees used to have acorns / but now teacups fall gently . . ."

It's the nature of poetry, your own included, to begin to mean something *after a while.* This is puzzling, and suspiciously Zen-like, but it has to do with the way we read it. (The wonderful poet Josephine Jacobsen says that poetry works "by long-term osmosis.") Poetry mirrors the world, as a tree does, or a cloud. This was Tennyson's insight in his poem, "Flower in the Crannied Wall": holding the little flower in his hand, the speaker observes, "but *if* I could understand/What you are, root and all, and all in all,/I should know what God and man is."

In this spirit, a patient reader can find aspects of "Teacups" to empathize with, and understand. It's a funny situation. One speaker is a klutz, the other a lot sharper. This poem describes a domestic scene (kitchen, bedroom) in which vague and very polite parents are pushed around by their children, who take the new order—teacups falling out of trees—in stride. Both in writing and reading poetry, you have to go with what is given.

What I wanted to demonstrate here was my earlier point. Poems don't have to mean anything; the meaning will take care of itself. I wasn't thinking of meaning anything when I wrote "Teacups." I *did* try to link sounds that worked together: bedroom/branches/broken; acorns/porcelain/bourbon; tea/*cherie*/trees; cries/lives; everywhere/dears. And a rhythm that staggered unpredictably, like the parents, ending with a kind of satisfactory karate chop: Take that, sweeties!

The last line, "Rake up those goddam teacups," is almost a punch line, which reminds me of Howard Nemerov's comparison of poetry with jokes: You either "get" the joke or you don't; no amount of explanation will make it work. But here we're looking at poems the way comedians look at jokes, as professionals or at least serious amateurs, trying to understand what succeeds, and why.

Three main points to remember: 1) Meaning isn't the main attribute of a poem, but a good poem will tend to mean something whether intentionally or not. 2) Clarity is still a virtue, even though sometimes it's the "meaningless" clarity of dreams; deliberate or careless obscurity is still a vice. And 3) Like a pool, a good poem can be both mysterious and transparent; in this context "difficulty" is irrelevant. We don't think of pools as difficult.

𝕊. 4

The Shape of Poetry

IN RECENT YEARS, many people have become attracted to what's called the New Formalism—the work of poets like Julia Alvarez, Tom Disch, Dana Gioia, Marilyn Hacker, Rachel Hadas, Andrew Hudgins, Sydney Lea, Brad Leithauser, Molly Peacock, Wyatt Prunty, Mary Jo Salter, and others. Several good anthologies of formal verse have proved popular; for example, *Strong Measures*, edited by Philip Dacey and David Jauss, and *Rebel Angels*, edited by Mark Jarman and David Mason.

American poetry goes in waves and counter-waves, and the New Formalism is a reaction/rebellion against the dominance of free verse, which has been ascendant since the fifties. Allen Ginsberg's *Howl* (1956), Robert Lowell's *Life Studies* (1959), and Adrienne Rich's *Necessities of Life* (1966) can be taken as the conquering free-verse flagships. For a while in the sixties and seventies many editors refused even to consider rhymed poetry, which was looked upon either as a slick attribute of advertising jingles or a politically conservative statement. Poet Diane Wakoski denounced all poets working in form as "Eurocentric."

But the revival of interest in form is a good development. Form is no more Eurocentric than Robert Frost is.

Poets should know what form has to offer. They should be able to recognize which forms might be compatible with their talents, just as painters and musicians benefit from working with a variety of materials. The poet is a composer and should be able to call in the oboes, the drums, the trumpets—the various instruments available.

But New Formalism is not an interesting subject in itself, because it's irrelevant to the main question: Are the poems good or not? Writing a villanelle or a sonnet is neither a virtue nor a sin. The point is, does it work? Just as "free verse" often disguises laziness of thought and execution, "formal verse" often sugarcoats a bloodless triviality.

My thesis in this chapter is simple: I think every poem, formal or free, has an ideal shape, and the job of the poet is to find it. (Perhaps this is partly what Gerard Manley Hopkins meant by his term "inscape"—the "pattern" of a poem.) These shapes are limitless, but I believe some poems want to be free and all over the page, and some want to be haiku or sestinas. A good poem has a mind of its own.

A poet working on early drafts has to recognize which way the poem is leaning. Of course, to do that you have to be familiar with the possibilities. No one can write poetry who doesn't spend a lot of time studying it.

The *subject* of a poem doesn't matter; in fact, the ostensible subject—rose, apple, teacup—often turns out not to be the subject at all. What's interesting in a poem is its invention, freshness, approach—the way the poet's mind works. Auden, whose subjects included everything from love to capitalism, called a poem essentially "a verbal contraption."

Here's the title poem of one of my books:

Liquid Paper

Smooth as a snail   this little parson
pardons our sins   Touch the brushtip
lightly and   *abracadabra!*   a clean slate

We know those who blot their brains
by sniffing it   which shows
it erases more than ink
and with imagination anything
can be misapplied . . .   In the army
our   topsergeant   drank aftershave   squeezing
my Old Spice to the last slow drop

It worked like Liquid Paper in his head

until he'd glide across the streets of Heidelberg
hunting for the house in Boise Idaho
where he was born . . .   If I were God
I'd authorize Celestial Liquid Paper
every seven years to whiten our mistakes:
we should be sorry and live with what we've done
but seven years is long enough and all of us

deserve a visit now and then
to the house where we were born
before everything got written so far wrong

(first published in *The New Virginia Review*)

In the first few drafts of this poem, it was all in one
stanza, a regular (or irregular) free verse poem, about
half again as long as the final version. I think it's best to
write uncritically until you come to a stopping point, or
run out of steam (I have a tendency to run right past the
real ending of a poem and have to cut the last lines).

When the first impulse of "Liquid Paper" was worked
out, I began to think about what would be the best structure for the poem. It was clear that although the lines
tended to be about the same length, it wasn't going to be

regularly rhymed or metered: no clusters of rhymes or near-rhymes looking to get organized, no iambic pentameter motor throbbing below the surface.

Soon, I noticed that the first line mentioning Liquid Paper was more or less in the middle, so I isolated it. Computers are very good for doing this sort of thing; I enjoy writing longhand and on my ancient Smith-Corona, but once I've got a decent draft, I put it on my computer and work from there.

The line, "It worked like Liquid Paper in his head," was now alone—like Liquid Paper itself, clearing a little space. It's also the only perfect iambic pentameter line. Dropping lines and phrases here and there, I shaped the poem so the same number of lines preceded and followed this central line.

Now I had a funny-shaped poem, with two stanzas of about a dozen lines surrounding a skinny one-line stanza. It was a little hard to read or to follow. I looked for the first natural break, which came after "a clean slate" in the third line, so I made that a three-line stanza. (That seemed right: it *was* a clean slate.) I then tried writing the poem with three-line stanzas—William Carlos Williams's favorite shape—surrounding the middle line. That wasn't bad, but it never quite worked. The poem didn't want to be in three-line stanzas. The breaks neither felt right nor made sense.

It took me a while to recognize that this was a poem with a religious thrust. I had begun just by staring at the familiar little black bottle with a white cap—it could just as well have been a pair of scissors or a paper clip—and seeing what I could think about it, where it would lead me. Gradually it took on the appearance of a tiny white-haired black-robed priest. When I realized that I had used the number "seven" twice, that led me to the symmetrical final shape of three/seven/one/seven/three—

those numbers all having religious significance (the Trinity, the Seven Deadly Sins, etc.).

The point about all this shifting around is to find the shape in which your poem most clearly and vividly expresses itself. Few readers will notice what you've done, just as no one can see the backbone that holds up your body, but it's important because it supports your poem.

One advantage of working in this way is that it's easier to know when your poem is finished. Although it may be true that poems are not so much finished as abandoned, there's a greater chance that the poem will *feel* finished when you put the last touches on a satisfactory shape.

As I stared at "Liquid Paper" in its final stages, I could see that in the (now) second stanza there was a leap of imagination between "misapplied" and "In the army"; and this was more or less balanced by a similar leap in the fourth stanza, between "born" and "If I were God." I wouldn't have noticed this if I hadn't already broken the poem down into these particular stanzas, but once I had, I worked on creating a mirror image, dropping a few words, and adding the ellipses (. . .), making a four/three: three/four split within the seven-line stanzas.

So, does anyone care? I care, the way a painter may stare with dissatisfaction at her painting, and then add a little touch of red to the bottom left-hand corner and say, "That's it!" Though no one else may notice, the painter knows that she has finished her painting.

I hope when you first read "Liquid Paper" it seemed perfectly natural, as if this is just the way it popped out of my head. As Yeats wrote:

A line will take us hours maybe;
Yet if it does not seem a moment's thought,
Our stitching and unstitching has been naught.
                    (from "Adam's Curse")

As in an overcoat, the stitches—the work—in poems shouldn't show. Readers don't like to see the poet working; it's like watching a nervous comedian or actor, sweating and trying too hard. As Humpty Dumpty implied in *Through the Looking-Glass,* with language we need to show who's boss.

The sound of "Liquid Paper" is shaped, too—from the beginning alliterations to the combination at the end of "done," "long," "all," "then," "born," "wrong." Some of these were present in the first draft, but many were added, and much was jettisoned to highlight the sound that I saw already imbedded there.

I hope also that the poem sounds "true"; I think it's a true feeling. But some "facts"—as opposed to "truth"— had to be sacrificed for the shape of the sound. For example, my poor old sergeant did drink my Old Spice, and that fit well because "Old Spice" goes nicely with "misapplied." But I was stationed in Schweinfurt, not Heidelberg—and I think the sergeant was from Newark. Obviously, for all kinds of "sound" reasons, Heidelberg and Boise, Idaho, work a lot better here. "Until he'd stagger across the streets of Schweinfurt" and "hunting for the house in Newark, New Jersey" might have been "true," but the sound is so awkward it breaks up the thought.

There will always be disagreement between those who favor "spontaneity" and little rewriting (the beatnik poets, for example, or the late Frank O'Hara) and those who, like Yeats, "labor to be beautiful." Nothing wrong with that. Every poem is a mixture of lines that have just been "given" to us—the inspiration—and those that we have worked on to fulfill the promise of the original lines—the perspiration. Of course, we tend to be "given" more lines when we're well prepared. Allen Ginsberg, famous for his free verse, began by writing Blakean rhymed poems. As Alexander Pope wrote, "True ease in writing comes from art, not chance,/As those move easiest who have learned to dance."

If you're one of those poets whose lines (mostly) come out best on the first try—God bless. I'm jealous. And of course, this happens to everyone, even to me once in a while. But as advice to novices, I must say that ninety-nine percent of first drafts benefit from rewriting. Severe rewriting, serious shaping. An inspiration is not a poem, but with hard work and an eye to the shape it's struggling to be, you can make it become a poem.

Here's another, perhaps simpler, example. The source for this poem was a photograph, along with some notes I took during a trip to Italy—and a father's feeling for a daughter who had decided to live a continent away:

Soldiers With Green Leggings
Villa Schifanoia, 1987

Father and daughter marched between
the erect cypresses   moss turning

the dark trunks green
on the north side

like soldiers with green leggings
and he wanted to say

Let us lay down our swords
(how pompous like a father!)

and she wanted to say
Let's open our doors

(how sentimental like a daughter!)
but the music in their heads

kept playing so they held
their chins high   stepping

together left right left right
smart as any parade and soon

the trees marched with them
ground rumbling like distant cannon

birds whirling like bewildered
messengers until a white flag

rose from the castle
and they fell to their knees

to sign the treaty
any treaty: My treaty   Your treaty

(first published in *America*)

This poem went through many "shapes" until I came up with these couplets, marching unpunctuated in parade formation down the page, mirroring the two people in the poem. An early draft began like this:

Father and daughter walked by the dark
cypresses   moss turning the trunks green
on the north side   like soldiers with green
leggings   He wanted to say   Let us lay down our
     swords
and she wanted to say   Let us open our doors . . .

Changing it into couplets focused the poem and led to the parenthetical additions, as well as to other changes suggested by the new structure.

Now for a discussion about punctuation (I've already discussed my own idiosyncrasies). Poetry is the kind of writing in which everything's important: words, spaces, rhythms, line endings and beginnings, sound—and punctuation. Basically I advise you to *use normal grammar and punctuation,* because it's the most common contemporary style and therefore isn't obtrusive.

Many poets, like X. J. Kennedy, capitalize the beginning of each line:

You know it's April by the falling-off
In coughdrop boxes—fewer people cough—
By daisies' first white eyeballs in the grass
And every dawn more underthings cast off.

("B Negative")

Most contemporary poets, like Maxine Kumin, capitalize only the beginnings of sentences:

The poet, a hill man, curses
machinery.   Cars run over his dogs.
Tractors balk, slip into reverse
or threaten to tip over on the slopes.

("Night Soil")

Some poets develop punctuation idiosyncrasies like the small "i" for "I," for example, which is hard to use without reminding the reader of E. E. Cummings. In fact, Cummings's typographical experiments—"mOOn Over tOwns mOOn" or "Crowdloomroar:ing;diskface,es," etc.—make most similar efforts seem derivative, though it can be done, as in Robert Creeley's famous "I Know A Man":

drive, he sd, for
christ's sake, look
out where yr going.

W. S. Merwin, on the other hand, uses no punctuation at all:

In one of the dreams men tell how they woke
a man who can't read turned pages
until he came to one with his own story
it was air

                                        ("The Dreamers")

Some poets write little skinny poems, others are all
over the page, and many vary their practice from poem
to poem. Some poets would never think of using a semico-
lon. Many develop their own grammatical and punctua-
tional shorthands. One of the most interesting shapes
was practiced by poet/New Directions publisher James
Laughlin. He wrote on a typewriter, and each line would
deviate in length no more than two typewritten spaces
from the length of the first line. This strange system
(which, of course didn't "translate" exactly when typeset
in a book) worked very well for him!

The only real rule is to use what you think works best
for your own voice. Generally speaking, *you need less
punctuation in poetry than you do in prose,* because the
lines tend to be shorter and the ends of the lines create
natural pauses. When in doubt, leave it out.

I know that many young writers are bored by talk
about the shape of poetry or its attendant punctuation,
but this is a mistake. The great Romantic poet William
Blake once wrote, "Without *Minute Neatness of Execution*
the Sublime cannot Exist! Grandeur of ideas is founded
on Precision of Ideas." These technical decisions are not
superfluous to your poem, but intrinsic. They *are* your
poem. This is the kind of detail that separates poets from
journalists, lecturers, and philosophers.

ℬ. 5

Starting a Poem

MOST BEGINNING POETS don't have trouble starting a poem; you probably have started hundreds. It's *finishing* a poem that's difficult, and more challenging. But sometimes everyone gets stuck: the dread writer's block.

I no longer worry about this, knowing from experience that a little fallow time is sometimes needed, to let the soil rejuvenate. The Romantic poets had a favorite metaphor for creativity, the Aeolian harp—a harp with stretched strings often placed in windows so that when the wind blew, it would make music. Many of these poets looked upon themselves as writers who waited passively for inspiration to blow through them:

> And what if all of animated nature
> Be but organic Harps diversely framed,
> That tremble into thought, as o'er them sweeps
> Plastic and vast, one intellectual breeze,
> At once the Soul of each, and God of all?
>
> (from "The Eolian Harp," by Samuel Taylor Coleridge)

Well, we *are* harps, and inspiration is real, but we can fan the breeze a little ourselves. The first way is to relax and be patient. Something will come, the breeze will pick up again. To help this along, however, it's good to have a regular time and place for writing poems. Just as you can train yourself to remember dreams, you can train yourself to be receptive to the poetic ideas circulating around and inside you.

A notebook, as I've said before, can be a great help; just pick a phrase out of it, transfer it to your computer, or typewriter, or legal pad, and see what comes. The simple act of carrying a notebook around and writing in it can make you a more observant person, and more likely to write poetry. Poets are natural spies and eavesdroppers; they should be seers (see-ers), as well.

Figure out whether silence or music sparks your creative energy. I need silence before I can concentrate, but many writers prefer working while listening to music, usually classical. Hart Crane was famous for writing his poems to the strains of Ravel's "Bolero"; Frank O'Hara turned on Rachmaninoff concertos. I've known several city poets who couldn't write in the country: too quiet, or the birds and crickets bothered them.

Poetry can and does get written anywhere, and under any conditions. Some poets write standing up, some write in bed, many have written in prison, but it makes sense to help your writing along however you can. If you have a place where you regularly go to write—spending hours and hours in a room of your own—you should make it comfortable: a good chair at the right height to avoid back problems or carpal tunnel syndrome; a desk with enough room to spread out; a good light; a window (unless you're like Marcel Proust and prefer a cork-lined room); the usual supplies: pencils, pens, paper, envelopes, stapler, Scotch tape, scissors, calendar.

I have a file cabinet, which every poet needs after writing for several years: drafts, letters from editors, letters from writers, correspondence, articles to save, deadlines. The business of poetry churns out a lot of paperwork!

You may like some pictures or photos on your desk and walls. On my wall there's a blown-up photograph my wife took of Yeats's tombstone in Drumcliff churchyard: "Cast a cold eye / On life, on death. / Horseman, pass by!" Also on my wall is a James Thurber sketch of himself and a poster/photograph of my favorite artist, Camille Pissarro. A couple of beer coasters from Neuchatel protect the much-scarred desk from new coffee stains. It's far from plush, but it's comfortable; it's the place I go to write.

The need, as always, is to be able to clear your mind and concentrate, and try to sink deep within yourself to find the poem, which can appear from anywhere. Robert Frost said, "A poem begins as a lump in the throat, a sense of wrong, a homesickness, a lovesickness. . . . It finds the thought and the thought finds the word." Sometimes you can't control your surroundings, and you just have to give writing your best shot, from wherever you are.

Recipe

Let's say you want to write a poem
yes?
a good poem   maybe not The Second Coming but
your hair is getting thin already and
where's your Dover Beach?

Everything seems somehow out of reach
no?
all of a sudden everyone's walk-
ing faster than you and
you catch yourself sometimes staring not at girls

You live in at least two worlds
yes?
one fuzzy one where you always push
the doors that say pull and
one clear cold one where you live alone

This is the one where your poem is
yes?
no
It's in the other one
tear your anthologies into small pieces
use them as mulch for your begonias and
begin with your hands

(first published in Poetry)

This poem speaks for itself, but I can perhaps get it
to talk faster by saying a little about it. The image of the
poet isolated in his or her own world is pervasive in our
society: the "clear cold one where you live alone." And it's
true that for the most part, you're alone when writing.
But Yeats was right when he wrote, in "The Circus Animals' Desertion," "I must lie down where all the ladders
start, / In the foul rag-and-bone shop of the heart." That
is to say, poems should come from the crowded real
world, not the rarefied romantic one. And although you
should read as much as you can of the great poets who
have gone before you, if you hope to write poetry over any
length of time, you must also grow *out* of the anthologies
and find your own voice. Your poems must emerge from
your own experience, even—or perhaps particularly—
from your most painful experience. So "begin with your
hands" means you should 1) sit down and begin to write,
and 2) dig into the roots of your own life (the anthologies
will make excellent mulch).

"Recipe" also has a subliminal message: *Poetry is that
special language with which much care is taken.* Al-

though the lines may seem to be written in light chatty free verse, closer inspection will show it's not all that "free." Rhymes or near-rhymes link the stanzas (beach/ reach, girls/worlds, alone/poem). The next-to-last line of each stanza ends with the conjunction "and." A five-line structure is repeated up to the last stanza when the two-line reversal ("no/It's in the other one") extends that stanza to seven. Also notice the alliteration (cold/clear, begonias/begin), the odd hyphenation (walk-/ing), the dis-jointed sentence structure ("staring not at girls").

All of these details represent decisions I had to make, ideas I had, effects—successful or not—that I was con-sciously striving for while writing "Recipe." The reader shouldn't even be aware of them, at least not at first. But they're important. They make the poem a poem.

Your story is interesting to you because of what hap-pened. What will make your story interesting to others is the way you tell it. What you should always be looking for when starting a poem is finding and using fresh lan-guage. In "Recipe," the perky "yes/no" structure with its reversal was enough to get me going. Almost all poets have their "Writing a Poem" poem—there must be thou-sands of them!—so why add another? My job as a writer was to make it verbally lively, funny, sad, helpful—*worth reading*. Some poems aren't worth reading, just as, in a sense, some people aren't worth meeting, although these judgments and reactions vary widely with the individual. To make your poem readable, attack it, as you begin, with the same physical intensity and pleasure that a child uses working with Play-Doh, or building blocks, putting it together a handful at a time. The energy that goes into writing your poem will be the energy that shines out of it.

Many writers, finding themselves stuck, are able to get going again by concentrating on some ordinary object

around them. I might look out my window and describe
the live oak there. Two kinds of Spanish moss, hanging
and balled, cling to it. A limb looks dead. A bald patch is
spreading on the main trunk. One limb is much longer
than the others, reaching toward the sun; a bluejay on it
is eyeing a mockingbird with suspicion. I can say so much
about this tree! You can do the same with a waste basket
or a bottle of Liquid Paper or the wires leading to your
electric outlets. Poems begin with close observation, so
the act of describing something within view is a good exercise, and with luck and care, you can find yourself writing a real poem.

One other suggestion I should add about starting.
Write as fast as you can think and feel, uncritically, for
as long as you can. Just let it all flow out. See where the
poem's going, and try to get there. Afterwards, you can
take all the time you want to rewrite.

I mentioned before that I often write past the point
that I need to; when I reread what I've written, I see I've
repeated myself, or spelled out the obvious. Usually in
rewriting, my poems shrink. Of course, many poets don't
work that way. Apparently Dylan Thomas would labor
all morning on a single line, perfect it, and then head to
the pub. The next day, another line, and so on until a
poem was done. But most poets do it the other way
around: Write the first draft fast, then spend however
much time it takes on making a poem out of it.

Beginning a poem may be like diving into a strange
lake. You can look all you want, you can prepare all morning, you can study the water, you can stick your toe in,
but sooner or later you have to jump. This takes courage,
as does any important act that has no guarantee of a successful conclusion. Still, when you hit that water and look
around, there's nothing else quite so exciting.

With these thoughts in mind, we've perhaps arrived

at a good time to look at some of the more traditional shapes, or set forms, of poetry. In the next few chapters I'm going to discuss in detail some popular specific forms—the sonnet, syllabic poetry, the sestina, the pantoum, and the villanelle—because I've worked extensively in them. But much of what I say about one form will apply as well to another, and indeed to free verse. The need for music, passion, intelligence, and knowledge is always there, no matter how it's displayed. As Adrienne Rich observed in her collection of essays, *What Is Found There*, a traditional shape is "just a point of takeoff."

PART TWO: FORMS

ℬ. 6

Form and the Abecedarian

W HAT YOU STRIVE for in a formal poem is a basic
rhythm. Once that is "set," even lines that normally wouldn't "fit" just seem like an interesting variation. For example, "be<u>cause</u> the sun's <u>force</u>" (dimeter)
could be read as a three-beat line (trimeter)—"be<u>cause</u>
the <u>sun's</u> <u>force</u>"—but the basic two-beat rhythm of my
poem "Atomic Pantoum" pushes you to read it a little
faster:

> In a <u>chain</u> re<u>ac</u>tion
> the <u>neu</u>trons re<u>leas</u>ed
> <u>split</u> other <u>nu</u>clei
> which re<u>leas</u>es more <u>neu</u>trons . . .
>
> The <u>fish</u> catch on <u>fire</u>
> be<u>cause</u> the sun's <u>force</u>
> in a <u>chain</u> re<u>ac</u>tion
> has <u>blazed</u> in our <u>minds</u> . . .

Counting beats and measuring meters is an art more
than a science. Most lines may be read in several different ways, with different emphases. But establishing a
basic meter helps the writer control the way a poem is
read. Though you don't need to use the formal nomencla-

ture very often, the following are the names of the most common meters used to measure poetic lines; unless otherwise indicated, the quotes are from poems of mine:

Monometer (one beat):

Where have
you gone,
my love?
Moon on
our wet
street burns
without
you

(from David Baker's "Sonnet for a Separation")

Dimeter (two beats):

Blind to the end
we sing to Jesus
in a chain reaction . . .

Because the sun's force
with plutonium trigger
has blazed in our minds
we're dying to use it

(from "Atomic Pantoum")

Trimeter (three beats):

Bones in an African cave
gave the show away:
they went violent to their grave . . .

(from "Bones in an African Cave")

Tetrameter (four beats):

The angel of the Lord sang low
and shucked his golden slippers off
and stretched his wings as if to show . . .

(from "The Gift of the Magi")

Pentameter (five beats):

A monk can do his work on bended knees
inside or out; the bishop looked askance
when Mendel labored in a row of peas

(from "Mendel's Laws")

Hexameter (six beats), also called the Alexandrine:

Confusion of the death-bed over, is it sent
Out naked on the roads, as the books say, and stricken
By the injustice of the skies for punishment?

(from William Butler Yeats's "The Cold Heaven")

Though for the most part, **heptameter (seven beats)** has pretty much disappeared since Rudyard Kipling's "The Ballad of East and West," in a recent issue of *The Times Literary Supplement* (London) I found a poem by Glyn Maxwell called "Deep Sorriness Atonement Song," that begins:

The man who sold Manhattan for a halfway decent
    bangle,
He had talks with Adolph Hitler and could see it from
    his angle . . .

Similarly, **octameter (eight beats)** is also very rare. Most of you know it from Edgar Allan Poe's "The Raven":

Once upon a midnight dreary, while I pondered, weak
    and weary,
Over many a quaint and curious volume of forgotten
    lore . . .

Obviously, you can break the heptameter line into one tetrameter and one trimeter line, and the octameter into two tetrameter lines, both of which combinations are very common; this can give similar—though not exactly the same—effects.

Poetry isn't analysis, but if you're going to be a serious poet, you should take the time to learn the terms and tools of your trade, and then more or less forget about them until you need them.

"Form," wrote the critic Kenneth Burke, "is a satisfied expectation." One way to start writing formal poetry is with the "easiest" of forms—the abecedarian, an acrostic form in which you write the alphabet down the left-hand side of the page, and fill in the poem. It's more difficult than that, of course, particularly as you near the end of the alphabet. One way to do it is to *overdo* it, to show who's boss, as Gavin Ewart does in "The Statements": "Arts are actually anthropomorphic./ Business is often bilaterally baleful./Causality is a considerable cow . . ." etc. You can write the poem backward from Z to A, and even rhyme it, as in Tom Disch's delightful "Zewhyexary": "Z is the Zenith from which we decline, / While Y is your yelp as you're twisting your spine . . ." Here's one of mine that turns on our current exercise craze:

The ABC of Aerobics

Air seeps through alleys and our diaphragms
balloon blackly with this mix of
carbon monoxide and the thousand corrosives a city
doles out free to its constituents
Everyone's jogging through Edgemont Park
frightened by death and fatty tissue
gasping at the maximal heart rate
hoping to outlive all the others streaming
in the lanes like lemmings lurching toward their last
jump   I join in despair
knowing my arteries jammed with
lint and tobacco   lard and bourbon: my

medical history a noxious marsh
Newts and moles slink through the sodden veins
owls hoot in the lungs' dark branches
Probably I shall keel off the john like
queer Uncle George and lie on the bathroom floor
raging about Shirley Clark   my true love in
seventh grade   God bless her wherever she lives
tied to that turkey who hugely
undervalues the beauty of her tiny earlobes   one
view of which (either one: they are both perfect)
would add years to my life   and I could skip these
x-rays   turn in my insurance card   and trade
yoga and treadmills and jogging and zen and
zucchini for drinking and dreaming of her   breathing hard

(first published in *Sun Dog*)

Every poem must work *on its own terms*, and must succeed *as a poem*, whether free verse, limerick, villanelle, or abecedarian. The question to ask yourself, always, is why should people read this? What's in it for them? It can be different aspects—a feeling of pleasure or of recognition or shock or sadness, which can come from either *what* is said, or *how* it's said; and in the best poems, from both.

I wanted "The ABC of Aerobics" to seem fast on its feet, to exaggerate the alphabet by doubling and tripling a lot of the letters, even the Z ("zen and/zucchini"), but I also wanted it to tell a story that would interest readers enough to make them forget about the form as the poem moved along. Form should be an open window through which the reader looks at the scene described. Here it's a "lost love" story, in which the speaker's thoughts about the health benefits of jogging lead him to consider mortality and his old sweetheart, until at the end he's "breathing hard," though not from aerobic exercising.

When you're writing in a specific form, keep in mind that the form doesn't excuse you from working on all the other elements that go into making a poem: rhythm, diction, image—the overall sound and sense. Just because you have the lines rhymed properly, or as in "Aerobics," you've fulfilled the alphabetical pattern, doesn't mean you have a poem yet. You still have to go through it, read it out loud, smooth the awkward spots, clarify what's murky, energize what's lax. Charles Wright, in *Written in Water, Written in Stone*, says, "In poems, all considerations are considerations of form." This is true even with poets who use free verse in the so-called flat style, where the emphasis is on tightness of image and intensity of insight rather than on repeated rhythms:

> Listen:
> the poets laureate live in a world
> of plants whose names we're not likely to say.
> But the roads I love
> lead to weed-thronged gullies . . .
>
> (from "Lemon Trees" by Reginald Gibbons

or

> Still at the gauze of dawn
> birdsong arouses
> feathers and bone,
> even you to the touch . . .
>
> (from "Habits of Love" by Jean Hollander)

You can see the alliteration of the "l" sounds in "Lemon Trees," the graceful grouping of sound-related phrases ("gauze of dawn"/"feathers and bone" in "Habits of Love." *We human beings have a natural love of order*, of objects or relationships that please our sense of organization and fulfillment.

We are also innately attracted to the orderliness of numbers (and one of the definitions of "numbers" is "metrical structure," as in Longfellow's famous "Tell me not, in mournful numbers, /Life is but an empty dream!").

Students often object to formal poetry because they think it's not "natural," like free verse, which is looser and less regimented. And yet the sun rises and sets, the moon and the planets wheel around, the seasons come and go, according to their strict schedules. Snowflakes, flowers, shells, spider webs appear as hexagons, spirals, sequences of mathematical purity. The heart bumps along in iambic regularity. We're surrounded, indeed engulfed, by naturally repeating forms.

One common objection to writing formal poetry rather than free verse is that it's harder to do. Of course, *good* free verse is also hard to write, but free verse is much more difficult to judge. It's easier to spot awkward rhythms or forced rhymes in a sonnet than to see just what's wrong with many free verse poems.

Generally, aspiring poets should begin with free verse, but, gradually (and soon), as they develop their strengths, they should begin to explore the possibilities of formal poetry. Read sonnets by Donald Justice and Richard Wilbur, sestinas by Elizabeth Bishop and Dana Gioia, pantoums by Marilyn Hacker and John Ashbery, villanelles by Dylan Thomas and Theodore Roethke. Start experimenting on your own.

I believe beginning poets can improve their writing by experimenting with formal poetry, learning in this way to solve the various technical problems that inevitably crop up, no matter what kind of poetry they're writing. And you should be ready to write a sonnet or sestina when the right combination of subjects and rhythms comes to mind.

The real secret of poetry is "simply" *repetition with variation*. Readers and listeners have different "ears" for rhythm, and one poet's cadences will not please everyone.

But it's essential for you to develop a rhythm more or less your own, which again will greatly depend on what moved you to write poems in the first place. Each of us has a unique "voice," and it's our job as poets to reveal this voice in writing. W. H. Auden, in his introduction to Constantine Cavafy's poems, wrote, "The conclusion I draw is that the only quality which all human beings without exception possess is uniqueness." This unique-ness often shows in the rhythms of our writing (whether free verse or formal patterns). This is why formal struc-tures by different writers don't sound at all alike.

"Rhythm," in the dictionary, is defined as *"regular* re-currence or alternation" (italics mine) and "a regular pat-tern formed by a series of notes of differing stress and duration." In "Aerobics," even though it's in "free verse" (except for the alphabetic structure), certain rhythms, or measures, are repeated over and over: "Air seeps through alleys," "carbon monoxide," "hoping to outlive," "knowing my arteries," "queer Uncle George," "yoga and tread-mills" all have similar beats. Many of the lines begin with participles: "gasping," "hoping," "raging." Repeating rhythmic structures is a major way to make free verse musical, as you can see in reading Walt Whitman:

> Out of the cradle endlessly rocking,
> Out of the mocking-bird's throat, the musical shuttle,
> Out of the Ninth-month midnight . . .
>   ("Out of the Cradle Endlessly Rocking")

It's just this kind of repetition that makes many read-ers consider much of the Bible to be poetry:

> And God said, "Let there be light," and there was
> light. And God saw that the light was good; and
> God separated the light from the darkness. God
> called the light Day, and the darkness he called

Night. And there was evening and there was
morning, one day.

(Genesis 3–5)

But it's not only free verse that needs to be musical.
Poetry at its best includes the pleasures of music, and no
matter what form you're working with, you need to keep
in mind that form is one thing and music is another, although they'll be fused together. Edgar Allan Poe's definition of poetry—"the rhythmical creation of beauty"—is
still one of the best.

One final note on the acrostic form: It's often used for
love poetry, as a present or valentine. Chaucer, Boccac-
cio, Villon, and Poe are some of the poets who used acros-
tics for this purpose, writing letters down one side of the
page to spell the loved one's name. (Conversely, this form
can be used effectively for hate poems, as well, as shown
in *Tygers of Wrath*, a marvelous anthology of very angry
poetry, edited by X. J. Kennedy.)

So, having said all this by way of introduction to
forms, let's move along to the most common one, the one
that almost every poet has written at one time or another—the sonnet.

🎜 7

The Sonnet

SONNETS ARE traditionally broken into two stanzas: the first eight lines—the octet—make a statement or set up a situation, and the final six lines—the sestet—turn it around or look more deeply into it, and come to a conclusion, or at least some kind of resolution.

The two most common rhyme schemes are the Petrarchan (or Italian) sonnet—abbaabba cdcdcd—and the Shakespearean (or English) sonnet—ababcdcd efefgg. The Shakespearean is probably the more common of the two in English because it's easier to rhyme (no quadruple rhymes!), and uses the couplet for a kind of snap ending: "So long as men can breathe, or eyes can see, / So long lives this, and this gives life to thee" (Sonnet 18). This can be a strength or a weakness, depending on how good you are at epigrammatic writing. Even Shakespeare's sonnets sometimes seem to consist of 1) the poem, and 2) the couplet summing up the poem.

The sonnet form also lends itself to sequences. Sir Philip Sidney, Edmund Spenser, and Shakespeare wrote sonnet sequences in the sixteenth century (following the great Italian poets Dante and Petrarch), and poets are still writing them today—for example Julia Alvarez's book-length sonnet sequence, *33*. The sonnet is a remark-

ably flexible form. Some excellent—and vastly different—sequences are Elizabeth Barrett Browning's *Sonnets from the Portuguese*, Edna St. Vincent Millay's *Fatal
Interview*, Rilke's *Orpheus Sonnets*, and Judson Jerome's
Partita in Nothing Flat.

Two things to say right away: 1) The sonnet is neither
old-fashioned nor dead; it's alive and well. Bright and
powerful sonnets are being published today in magazines
as widely apart in focus, readership, and geography as
The New Yorker and *The State Street Review* (Jackson-
ville, Florida). And 2) The sonnet's enduring popularity
and its ability to revitalize itself out of its own ashes as
regularly as the phoenix is no accident.

The sonnet fits the English language the way the
haiku fits Japanese and Chinese. The haiku in English,
with few exceptions, always seems a bit truncated; the
reader nods, but wants more. It's a better match for the
more pictorial oriental languages, with their built-in
symbol codes that add great density to each syllable. But
the sonnet's fourteen-line pattern has proved to be an excellent length in which an English or American poet can
develop an idea, turn it around, and bring it to a satisfactory conclusion.

Scholars disagree as to what, precisely, a sonnet is.
Originally, it meant "little song," and some poets still
hold to this: Ted Berrigan wrote an entire book of short,
unrhymed poems with a varying number of lines and different line lengths, called *Sonnets*.

But for our purposes we'll consider fourteen-line
poems of various rhyme schemes, usually in iambic pentameter (five-beat) lines, though there are myriad and
wonderful variations on this. Brad Leithauser and David
Baker both have written monometer sonnets; Leithauser's has one-syllable lines but the requisite fourteen lines

and traditional Petrarchan rhyme scheme, beginning
with the quatrain:

Why   (a)
do   (b)
you   (b)
sigh, (a)
      ("Post-Coitum Tristesse: A Sonnet")

Here's a poem of mine that combines sonnets with the
abecedarian:

Black Holes & Einstein

... First   they're marble-pale
as Venus   flicked in galactic flight
by the thumb of God   (you can see a Thumbnail
creasing the curved sky on velvet nights)
Disbelieving the hole's odd behavior
Einstein bet   despite his thirty years'
failure to reconcile stone and star
God wouldn't play dice with the universe

He thought the holes too random: our sky
is no lunar love nest or cosmic
jackpot where chips fall where they will   But why
kaleidoscoping through charged fields like shots
lagged in the void   do stars collapse and die
making a coffin of space so black and blocked

not even light can escape?   Though now it seems
out of this darkest deck   this dense egg
particles spin like roulette wheels   wild beams
quarks electrons   forming   a spectral peg
reuniting the universe   fusing
supernova with atom   star with stone
telling us there's   a rule for everything
under the sun: and everything beyond

Venus   green-eyed guide   dealer of hands   below
whose shaded light more dangerous than

x-rays we study the mysteries   if only
  you would illumine   (for us   for Einstein)
  Zeus and zero-zero   blind luck   black holes
    and if God's a gambling man . . .
                        (first published in *The Tampa Review*)

This poem uses a combination of *Shakespearean* rhyme scheme for the octet (abab cdcd); and *Petrarchan* for the sestet (cdcdcd). About halfway through the third or fourth draft, I realized I had various rhymes that could lend themselves to a double-sonnet, and then, when I split it, I noticed the scientific/mythic words beginning with odd letters: quarks, kaleidoscope, zero-zero, Venus, x-rays—and this gave me the idea of combining a double sonnet (28 lines) with an abecedarian (26 lines). Indenting the first and last lines solved the two-line disparity problem.

Talk at our dinner table often revolves around scientific topics, which naturally move into my poems, just as a meeting with your mechanic, your clergyman, or your doctor, with all their specialized vocabularies, can result in intriguing insights, phrases, and ideas. Subjects have to grab you, rather than the reverse. I don't think a poem works if you say, O.K., today I'm going to write a sonnet about grasshoppers, or Bosnia, or sonic booms. Although you can write about anything that interests you, the motivating force—the *passion*—you have for the subject must show through. This passion is hard to "work up"; it has to be there from the beginning.

To me, black holes—collapsed stars with their light "permanently" trapped inside—are fascinating, and a lot of what I've read about them is contradictory and confusing. "Black Holes & Einstein" is an exploration and an experiment in several ways to see what I thought, within the framework of the fused forms.

When you start thinking hard about something, other ideas soon get pulled into the mix. It's the way our minds, and poetry, work. So, thinking about the randomness of black holes led me to remember Einstein's famous quote, "God wouldn't play dice with the universe." That led to the concept of gambling in general and to playing marbles when I was a kid in Brooklyn (we used to "lag"—shoot—marbles toward a crack in the sidewalk). That in turn made me think of God playing marbles with the stars and planets, and eventually of Venus and thoughts of love, the greatest gamble of all. Very soon, I had more than enough to write about.

Because I was dealing with an abecedarian as well as with a double sonnet, I had no idea at the outset where this poem would go. The form itself—the letters of the alphabet and the rhyme scheme—moved me along. Howard Nemerov has said that one great advantage of form is that it makes you smarter than you are. With free verse you're on your own, with your own ideas, there for you to explore.

But most of us don't have that many original or interesting ideas, which is why so much free verse is boring. There's nothing new in it. Form, however, although restrictive in some ways, has a mind of its own, and this gets grafted on to yours. You're looking for a rhyme or a rhythm; you have to condense or expand (usually condense) within its strictures. With luck, you come up with something new.

In "Black Holes," the idea of the universe being held together by quarks like "spectral pegs" would never have come to me on my own. Nor would the ending, combining myth and science, Zeus and "zero-zero" (the term for atmospheric conditions reducing visibility to zero). The ideas in this poem were shaped by the form, not by me.

The traditional rhythm of the sonnet is iambic pen-

tameter, and I use it as my base rhythm ("But <u>why</u> / ka-
<u>leidoscoping</u> through <u>charged fields</u> like <u>shots</u> / <u>lagged</u> in
the <u>void</u> do <u>stars</u> col<u>lapse</u> and <u>die</u> . . ."), but with lots of
variation.

Serious poets have to learn the difference between
iambic rhythms ("though <u>now</u> it <u>seems</u>"), trochaic
("<u>Venus Green</u>-eyed"), anapestic ("by the <u>thumb</u>" / "in the
<u>void</u>"), dactylic ("<u>lagged</u> in the" / "<u>making</u> a") and spon-
daic ("<u>blind luck black holes</u>")—to use two-beat examples
of the major poetic feet.

Here's a short list of the most-used metric feet (a
"foot" is the basic unit for measuring formal verse).

The two basic two-syllable feet are the **iamb** and the
trochee:

iamb: an iambic foot consists of an unaccented syllable followed by an accented one, as in "the <u>ball</u>" or "re-
<u>fuse</u>"

trochee: a trochaic foot consists of an accented syllable followed by an unaccented one, as in "<u>shoot</u> it" or
"<u>la</u>bor"

The two basic three-syllable feet are the **anapest** and
the **dactyl**:

anapest: an anapestic foot consists of two unaccented syllables followed by an accented one, as in "in the
<u>house</u>" or "inter<u>twine</u>"

dactyl: a dactylic foot consists of an accented syllable
followed by two unaccented ones, as in "<u>what</u> if a" or
"<u>happily</u>"

Two others, used occasionally, are the **pyrrhic** and
the **spondee**:

pyrrhic: a pyrrhic foot consists of two unaccented
syllables, as in "of a" or "in the"

spondee: a spondaic foot consists of two accented syllables, as in "blind luck" or "bread box"

Many fine books have been published on poetic form, including *The Longman Dictionary of Poetic Terms*, Laurence Perrine's *Sound and Sense*, and Lewis Turco's *The Book of Forms*. In his introduction, Turco observes, "One feature which distinguishes a poet from a versifier is that a poet *understands a pattern and works against it*, while a versifier *memorizes a pattern and works with it*" (italics his).

Other good books, which are also excellent anthologies, are John Frederick Nims's *Western Wind* and Robert Wallace and Michelle Boisseau's *Writing Poems*. Wallace's new book, *Free Verse and the Orbit of Meter*, argues that *all* verse in English is metrical and therefore measurable, even so-called free verse.

Advice on rhythm is double-edged: Learn the rules, the possibilities—and then break them. For example, "straight" iambic pentameter, or any rhythm pursued without variation, becomes rinky-tink very quickly. The rock musician Frank Zappa, speaking about music, said, "Without deviation from the norm, progress is not possible." This is true of writing sonnets, as well as other forms of poetry. Talking about the basic rhythmic structure of modern jazz and poetry, U.S. Poet Laureate Robert Pinsky put it this way: "To honor it, you have to change it a bit."

The same is true for rhyme. Besides making variations on traditional rhyme schemes like the Shakespearean sonnet, contemporary poets have long used "off-rhyme" (also called "near-rhyme" or "slant-rhyme") to create a modern, more conversational sound. Emily Dickinson was far ahead of her time when she wrote:

I taste a liquor never brewed—
From Tankards scooped in *Pearl*—
Not all the Vats upon the Rhine
Yield such an *Alcohol*!

> (#214: "I Taste A Liquor Never Brewed")

Her nineteenth-century editors wanted to change "Alcohol" to a purer rhyme, like "delirious whirl," but she held firm, put her poems in her closet, and waited for twentieth-century readers to welcome them.

Such flexibility opens up thousands more possibilities in rhyme, a great boon to poets. In "Black Holes," I use a lot of pure rhymes like "egg" and "peg," but I also rhymed "behavior" and "star," "years" and "universe," "shots" and "blocked," "stone" and "beyond." Sometimes you just have to suggest the rhyme: "below" and "only."

Here's a sonnet that consists mostly of off-rhymes, in no particular order:

In Gentler Times

In gentler times   if times were ever gentle
you'd blossom in a peasant blouse and dirndl
to linger by a stream below a windmill
while I would weave   upon my poet's spindle
bright cloth for your white shoulders   a gold mantle
of shining praise to cover love's old temple:
but now   my love   we know no such example
of hopeful days   if hope were ever ample

Today   hope stutters like a guttering candle
the dark too dark for love alone to handle
Godot   because unknown   is worse than Grendel
and love uncertain seems a certain swindle

And yet my love   our love's as quick to kindle
as simpler loves   if love were ever simple

> (first published in *The Antioch Review*)

Again, this is an example of bending the sonnet form and making it seem new. "In Gentler Times" is written in traditional iambic pentameter (the dark/too dark/for love/alone/to handle). To vary the rhythm, I have some run-on lines ("a gold mantle/of shining praise"; ". . .no such example/of hopeful days") where, instead of pausing at the end of the line, the reader is pulled along to stop somewhere in the next line. I've also inserted pauses (called "caesuras") at different points in the line to add to the variety within the basic rhythm (today//hope stutters/like a guttering/candle).

Like "In Gentler Times," sonnets have been, historically, love poems, but are by no means required to be. Think of Wordsworth's great sonnet that begins:

> The world is too much with us; late and soon,
> Getting and spending, we lay waste our powers:
> Little we see in Nature that is ours;
> We have given our hearts away, a sordid boon!

("The World is Too Much with Us")

John Donne's "Death Be Not Proud," Shelley's "Ozymandias" and Keats's "On First Looking into Chapman's Homer" are also famous sonnets on subjects other than love. But love continues to be the sonnet's main subject.

With rhythm, the important point is that it should supply variation within basic regularity. The poet J. V. Cunningham has said that as far as he was concerned poetry was metrical writing. You don't have to agree with Cunningham completely to realize that rhythm (*regular recurrence*) and meter (*measured* rhythm) have to be major tools for anyone serious about writing poetry. This means that at some point you'll have to learn *prosody*, the study of the metrical structure of poetry.

This needn't be too frightening, because iambic meters, particularly tetrameter (four beats) and pentameter (five beats), recur naturally in our speech. Our subject-verb order (he <u>ran</u>, I <u>jumped</u>, you <u>hid</u>) and our use of articles and possessives (the <u>girl</u>, a <u>boat</u>, her <u>book</u>) are iambic. So a normal conversation could be in iambic pentameter:

"I'd <u>like</u> an<u>oth</u>er <u>cup</u> of <u>cof</u>fee, <u>please</u>."
"I'm <u>very</u> <u>sorry</u> <u>but</u> we <u>close</u> at <u>five</u>."
"<u>OK</u>, but <u>can</u> I <u>have</u> a <u>cup</u> to <u>go</u>?" etc.

or in iambic tetrameter:

"I <u>won</u>der <u>where</u> my <u>wal</u>let <u>is</u>?"
"It's <u>on</u> the <u>dress</u>er, <u>id</u>iot!"
"Well <u>how</u> was <u>I</u> sup<u>posed</u> to <u>know</u>?" etc.

Poet Marilyn Nelson has used this as a class exercise, and in a few minutes the whole class was speaking in iambic pentameter.

My concluding example is a contradiction in terms: a free-verse sonnet. Of course, from any strict definition, this isn't a sonnet at all, just a fourteen-line poem; but I couldn't have written it this way, with its octet/sestet structure, if I hadn't spent a lot of time reading and writing sonnets. A study of form, in other words, will *in*form the rest of your writing, even your free verse, and help make it tighter and more effective.

The Heart's Location

all my plans for suicide are ridiculous:
I can never remember the heart's location
too cheap to smash the car
too queasy to slash a wrist
once jumped off a bridge
almost scared myself to death

then spent two foggy weeks
waiting for new glasses

of course I really want to live
continuing my lifelong search
for the world's greatest unknown cheap restaurant
and a poem full of ordinary words
about simple things
in the inconsolable rhythms of the heart

(first published in *Southern Voices*)

𝒮. 8

Syllabic Poetry

WITH SONNETS, and most formally patterned poems, we measure the line by counting its metric feet: iambic pentameter (five iambic feet), for example, or trochaic tetrameter (four trochaic feet). But you should know about another major formal way of ordering your poems—syllabic poetry—before moving into the more esoteric forms.

Syllabic poetry is measured by counting *every* syllable in a line, not just stressed syllables. In contrast, a pentameter line, with its five "beats," or stressed syllables, can have lots of different syllable counts, from five to fifteen or more. Here are some typical pentameter examples, all from Shakespeare:

> He that cuts off twenty years of life (9 syllables, *Julius Caesar*)
> Never, never, never, never, never! (10, *King Lear*)
> How weary, stale, flat, and unprofitable (11, *Hamlet*)
> O happy horse, to bear the weight of Antony! (12, *Antony and Cleopatra*)
> O Romeo, Romeo! Wherefore art thou Romeo? (14, *Romeo and Juliet*)

The advantages of syllabic poetry are three-fold: 1) It doesn't have to be rhymed, although it can be; 2) because every syllable counts, it tends to break up the regular iambic line, making for a more "contemporary" sound; and 3) it's a flexible form, perhaps the closest to free verse, as Marianne Moore has shown, with her stanzas consisting of alternating short and long syllable counts. Her poem "The Steeple-Jack," for example, is written in thirteen stanzas of six lines each; in the first stanza, she sets up a syllable count of 11/10/14/8/8/3, and pretty much sticks with that throughout all thirteen stanzas. I say "pretty much" because Moore wasn't a purist, and avoided what she called "conscious fastidiousness." In other words, *she* was the boss, not her syllabic scheme.

The syllabic form with which most aspiring poets are familiar is the Japanese haiku, or hokku, a seventeen-syllable poem: three lines of 5, 7, 5 syllables. True Japanese haiku always include a reference to a particular season, and consist almost entirely of images from nature, as this one by its most famous seventeenth-century practitioner, Basho:

> Evening darkens. Hunched
> On a withered bough, a crow.
> Autumn in the air.

In Japanese, these natural images have symbolic weight based on long cultural, literary, and religious traditions. In English they seem thinner and less satisfactory, so poets have tended to string them together in a series, as in Amy Lowell's "Twenty-Four Hokku On A Modern Theme," which begins, "Again the larkspur / Heavenly blue in my garden. / They, at least, unchanged"—and then goes on to tell a love story. Wallace Stevens's famous "Thirteen Ways of Looking at a Blackbird" is clearly haiku-influenced: "Among twenty snowy mountains, / The only moving thing / Was the eye of the blackbird."

Writers like Jack Kerouac distinguished the American haiku from the Japanese, giving it more license to vary the number of syllables. In his words, "I don't think American Haikus should worry about syllables because American speech is something again . . . bursting to pop." That's probably good advice, though the result may not be haiku, but just short three-lined poems.

Because it gives the poet a little more room, the Japanese tanka—an extended haiku with five lines totaling 31 syllables (5/7/5/7/7)—works better in English, as in the graceful series, "Petals on a Burning Pond" by contemporary poet Steven Lautermilch, which has this beautiful ending:

Full moon. Over the
valley the torchfall of stars
setting the shingled
roof aflame. The grass script of
this heart was paper and smoke.

The cinquain, a five-line poem with 2/4/6/8/2 syllables in succession, is an American offshoot of the tanka, invented by poet Adelaide Crapsey, but it never caught on, though several poets have made good use of it, as in this one by Babette Deutsch:

The Soul

Go thou
Her changing roads.
Know all her provinces.
Yet to her far frontiers thou shalt
Not come.

But most syllabic poetry in English establishes a set number of syllables per line and doesn't vary; the poem is sometimes broken into stanzas and sometimes not. Here's one of mine, written with eleven syllables per line:

Noreen

In any group there are the beautiful and
the plain   the strong & weak   smart as a trinket
& dumb as a clam   Agreed   But there's little
agreement who they are or correlation
with how they all turn out   Noreen here   lying

on the storeroom floor with her head on a sack
of potatoes   phone dangling from the wall and
a plastic cup of vodka on the shelf   was
voted Wittiest in the Class and the Girl
with the Nicest Eyes   *Where be your gibes now?*   asked

Hamlet as indeed did Noreen when playing
Hamlet in ninth grade   pronouncing it *guybs* while
Miss Endicott rolled her eyes which weren't half
as nice as Noreen's   Outside it's been dead cold
and rainy for a month and polluted air

gums your glasses like snails   the ink smears on her
lover's letter   *Dear Noreen*   For years she has
held the wrong job   the wrong man   She even had
the wrong child   Those are the reasons   How much we
need reasons!   How reasons make us feel better!

(first published in *The New Republic*)

"Noreen," a meditation about a person who was full of promise when young, but whose life inexplicably fell apart, was written first in free verse:

In every group
there are the beautiful and the plain
the strong and the weak
those smart as a trinket and dumb as a clam
But there is no agreement about

who they are or much correlation
with how they all turn out . . .

I saw the poem had to be tighter, better organized;
writing it syllabically showed me where the middle of the
poem was—*Where be your gibes now?*—and helped me
eventually to make four five-line stanzas. It also pushed
me into the repeated exclamations of the ending which
gives the poem the intensity it needs:

. . . Those are the reasons. How much we
need reasons!   How reasons make us feel better!

The last sentence ("How reasons . . .") came about almost entirely because the poem was eight syllables short,
and something needed to be added. This may sound
overly mechanical, but it's not: The syllabic form gave me
the opportunity to say what I wanted to say, *and showed
me how to do it.*

All poems don't need to be in stanzas, but, in general,
stanzas help clarify the meaning of a poem by separating
its major parts. Everything in poetry is important, even
the spaces between lines. A stanza break slows the reading down and enables the reader to "catch up" with the
various events that are taking place within the poem.

In creating stanzas, what you should look for first are
the natural breaks in a poem, and then, if possible, you
try to regulate them, to give a feeling of control and logical or emotional progress. The stanza breaks in "Noreen"
are pretty arbitrary, but I wanted to create the effect of
various stages in Noreen's life, beginning with youth and
moving up to the present, subliminally supporting the
progress of the poem from promise to breakdown.

Most of the time, in writing syllabics, the words
should fall into lines naturally, without using hyphens,

unless some particular word needs to be emphasized. Using hyphens calls attention to the form in an awkward way, as if it were a newspaper article. What you're looking for is a poem that seems (in the case of "Noreen") to fall easily into eleven-syllable lines, so you wouldn't want to write "play-/ing," "correl-/ation," or "trink-/et." You'll find that achieving this will require a lot of adjusting, a lot of close scrutiny, a lot of rewriting—but this will help improve your poem.

I rewrote the following poem over a hundred times, trying to get the right shape and syllabic count, finally solving the problem by using the title as the first word, and settling on five-line stanzas of 6/7/6/7/3 syllables:

Goalfish

are nomadic   slipping   (6)
sideways through shallows in tight   (7)
schools along shoreline breaks   (6)
to some warm shady weedbed   (7)
of our lake   (3)

They're serious   these goal-   (6)
fish   mouths frowning like bankers   (7)
heads shaking   eyes round as   (6)
nickels   *This is serious*   (7)
serious   (3)

When young the sweet darters
make easy prey   greengold scales
glinting like Spanish coins
translucent tails signaling
Swallow me

to the big fish cruising
and cashing in near deep holes
In winter even their
parents eat them as they flick
back and forth

under rock and dock   If
they survive   growing bars from
belly to fin   they'll do
the same to their own fry   sons
and   daughters

until time to move on	(6)
and they weave across borders	(7)
among hooks angling like	(6)
untranslated questions to	(7)
the slack at the end of the line . . .	(8)

(first published in *America*)

This poem began with a pun—goalfish for goldfish—
and observations of the small fish around our dock when
we lived for a few months on Lake Norman in North Car-
olina. Notice that the only hyphenated word is "goal-/
fish," used to emphasize the metaphor.

Most of the lines end naturally (end-stopped, or near
end-stopped, like "shoreline breaks," "shady weedbed,"
"greengold scales," "deep holes," etc.). In any form you
choose, keep in mind that besides the requirements of
that form, all other poetic devices still need to be considered. Here you can find examples of *alliteration*
(shoreline / shady), *rhyme* (rock /dock), *assonance*
(mouths / frowning), *consonance* (flick / back). In my rewriting I tried to emphasize the hard clicking sounds,
suggesting a hard conflicted life—"nomadic," "breaks,"
"lake," "nickels," "flick," "back," "rock," "dock"—ending in
"hooks" and "slack."

Gradually "Goalfish" developed into a satire on the
competitive pace of American life (big fish eat the little
fish), its greed and humorlessness (*"This is serious / serious"*). Paralleling Wordsworth's description in his "Im-
mortality Ode" ("Shades of the prison-house begin to
close / Upon the growing Boy"), I describe the surviving

fish as "growing bars from / belly to fin," which is accurate as a description of the fish as well as suggesting other and darker meanings.

Another important piece of general advice: Whenever you use specific objects, natural or unnatural, in your poems—apples, ships, worms, foxes, stars, magnets, teeth, fish—try to find more information, and particularly *a more specific vocabulary*, on that subject. You may find more precise words, new ideas; sometimes the whole poem might change because of information you find.

After I had sketched out "Goalfish," I looked up a few articles on small lake fish, like perch and bass, that I had recognized around our dock. A lot of the vocabulary (shoreline breaks, darters) and information on their behavior came from or was affected by what I read, especially the part about the parents eating their young, which fit perfectly into the general idea of the poem. *You can't have too much information about your subject.* After all, you don't have to use every bit, only what the poem needs.

One final note on "Goalfish." You may have noticed that the whole poem stays strictly in its 6/7/6/7/3 syllabic scheme until the very last line: "the slack at the end of the line." It's an ambiguous reference that could be taken several ways, depending on which meaning of "slack" you choose, but it seemed a good place to "slack off" from the strict syllable count and just let the line hang, which I did. I was having difficulty fitting the last stanza into the scheme—perhaps another example of Frost's idea of "taking advantage of happy accidents."

To summarize, syllabic poetry can give the poet a lot of freedom—like free verse cut up into arbitrary lengths—and still convey a feeling of control with the right subjects and suitable handling. The rhythm will vary from the common iambic and tend to follow the content or meaning almost conversationally, as in the darting feel of the fish "as they flick / back and forth // under rock and dock" in "Goalfish."

When a syllabic poem works, you have freedom fused to a particular kind of regularity, which sets up certain expectations and satisfactions. The best syllabic verse has something intriguing in each line, and therefore doesn't sound like cut-and-measured prose.

𝒮. 9

The Sestina

THE SESTINA was invented by a Provençal trouba-
dour named Arnaud Daniel in the twelfth century
and was "rediscovered" about twenty years ago, particularly in writing workshops; now some critics and writers
feel that it's been overdone, that too many "second-rate
sestinas" have been published.

This indicates to me just more of the usual disagree-
ments about what constitutes good poetry. After all, some
good editors liked these sestinas enough to publish them.
In any case, it's not the poet's job to be fashionable, or to
worry about what the editors are publishing, or the critics are frowning upon. The writer's job is to write as well
as he or she can, in whatever form suits the material
best. And sometimes that form is the sestina. If you have
a story circling in your mind, or in your notebook, if certain words keep popping up, the sestina may be the perfect form for what you want to say.

It's a difficult form, with even more of a mind of its
own than most other forms, perhaps because of its
length. A sestina consists of 39 lines: six six-line stanzas—hence its name—plus a three-line coda (a coda, or
envoy, is a closing formal refrain). The end-words (or *tel-
eutons*, from the Greek *telos*, meaning end) of the first six

lines are repeated in a set pattern, as if turned inside out, in the next five stanzas:

stanza:	1	2	3	4	5	6
end-words:						
1st line: **a**	f	c	e	d	b
2nd line:**b**	a	f	c	e	d
3rd line: **c**	e	d	b	a	f
4th line: **d**	b	a	f	c	e
5th line: **e**	d	b	a	f	c
6th line: **f**	c	e	d	b	a

Note that in a hypothetical seventh stanza, the end-words would circle back to their original order: a/b/c/d/e/f.   The last and first lines of each stanza are therefore joined by the same word being repeated: f/f, c/c, e/e, d/d, b/b.

In the three-line coda, the six end-words are repeated again. The "pure" sestina repeats them in this order: 1st line, b/e; 2nd, d/c; 3rd, f/a—thus the last end-word would be the same as the first line's end-word, giving a feeling of circularity. The rationale behind all this seems to have to do with the number "seven," the principle of change being multiples of seven: In the stanzas, the change each time (in line count) goes 6/1, 5/2, 4/3; in the coda, using the first stanza as guide, the numerical equivalents of the repeated end-words would be 5/2, 4/3, and 6/1.

But this is murky stuff indeed. In practice, the order of the words in the coda is often changed radically. Even in the main stanzas there are occasional variations. For example, in one of the most famous sestinas, Ezra Pound's "Sestina: Altaforte," in the fourth stanza the end-words of lines three ("rejoicing") and four ("music") are reversed—schematically, "music" should precede "rejoicing."

Although many poets use some form of syllabics these days, as I've mentioned, the sestina is somewhat out of fashion right now. Dana Gioia has written a very funny anti-sestina sestina, which includes these lines (stanzas 3 and 4):

Let's be honest. It has become a form for students,
an exercise to build technique rather than taste
and the official entry blank into the little magazines—
because despite its reputation, a passable sestina
isn't very hard to write, even for kids in workshops
who care less about being poets than contributors.

Granted nowadays everyone is a contributor.
My barber is currently a student
in a rigorous correspondence school workshop.
At lesson six he can already taste
success having just placed his own sestina
in a national tonsorial magazine . . .

("My Confessional Sestina")

But the sestina has particular attractions for poets writing in English because it takes advantage of certain characteristics of our language. English is a positional language; that is, many words can be used equally well as nouns, verbs, or adjectives, depending on where they are in the sentence. The sestina makes use of that flexibility, giving the repeated words variety. For example, you can say "This is a book" or "I'll book you" or "She's a bookworm," etc. A word's position in the sentence often shows the reader what part of speech it is. This makes it possible to repeat the end-words in many different variations.

In addition, English is full of homonyms (words pronounced and spelled alike but with different meanings, like "break" as a verb— "Don't break the vase"—or as a noun—"Give me a break") and homophones (words pronounced alike but spelled differently, like "break" and "brake," or "to," "too," and "two" in the following poem). In Anthony Hecht's moving sestina, "The Book of Yolek," the last line of the second stanza and the first line of the third illustrate the way it can work: "No one else knows where the mind wanders to. / / The fifth of August, 194<u>2</u>."

Here's a sestina of mine that should help explain this, as the end-words are the numbers one through six; you can see clearly how they evolve in the poem:

Warpath

Poets choose free verse over form   <u>one</u>
says   because they need room <u>to</u>
belt it out without stone-age <u>three</u>-
forked rules tomahawking their brains be<u>fore</u>
they get started   For example   the <u>five</u>
beat line has been passe since '5<u>6</u>

when *Howl* blasted its orgiastic <u>six</u>-
teen gun salvo to freedom without <u>one</u>
shot fired in reply (not counting <u>five</u>
or six palefaced rhymers trying <u>to</u>
hold the fort)   But any poetry   <u>for</u>-
mal or free   aims at making magic: <u>Three</u>

<u>snowy owls swooped down from the North on three</u>
<u>successive nights</u> and <u>That evening the six</u>-
<u>fingered Indian was dealing</u> and <u>I held four</u>
<u>queens at the stroke of midnight</u>   Everyone
knows that words   if they're right   are too
slick to be tied to any stake   <u>If</u>   I've

sometimes thought all theories are like the Five
Iroquois Tribes   ruling New York for three
or thirty or three hundred years   doomed to
dust sooner or later like rusty six-
guns   no one remembering who won
or lost   Only the words remain   neither for

nor against us   old arrowheads used for
paperweights   We can sing anything in five
beats or lines or syllables   even one
word is enough: Monongahela   And three
can make poetry   (Darkling I listen)   The critic sics
poets on each other like warring tribes to

his own greater glory   but the point is to
be able to tell your true story   formal as hell or completely free   in six
stanzas or none at all: to be able to say   Five
moons ago we touched under the tall three-
forked tree   and the wind and my heart were one

because in art   as in life   we should line up
our passions   single file   Indian style   with no
tricks: just one   two   three   four   five   six

(first published in *The Georgia Review*)

When I began this poem, I had no idea that the Indian
motif would develop. I just had some lines about poetry
that seemed to use a lot of numbers, so fairly early on I
thought I could try it as a sestina, and wrote out the end-
words of the stanzas to see what might happen; and
slowly Indian images began to appear, perhaps suggested by the rhyming combination of *Howl* and owl.

Once that happened, I began going back and picking
out verbs ("tomahawking"), nouns ("arrowheads"), and
adjectives ("palefaced") to support the metaphor. I even
found a five-syllable Indian word, "Monongahela," a river
in Pennsylvania, to fill out a line.

In *Poetic Diction: A Study in Meaning*, Owen Barfield
notes that the pleasure readers receive from poetry is at
least three-fold: 1) the pleasure from the poem itself, its
evidence of the poet's *individual* voice; 2) the pleasure
from the poem's shared or *collective* voice (Barfield calls
it "joint-stock poetry"), as in the characteristics shared

by metaphysical or Cavalier or beatnik poetry; and 3) the pleasure from the way the poet has handled the difficulties or problems arising from *the form itself*.

In other words, a large part of the enjoyment experienced from reading a sonnet or sestina comes from the reader's appreciation of the way the poet has "solved" it. We know this isn't "unpremeditated art," any more than a professional golfer's shot is the result of an unpracticed swing.

In writing "Warpath," my greatest pleasure came at the end, when the numbers were just waiting there and rolled out, making sense and even accidentally rhyming ("six" and "tricks"). I also enjoyed working out the "solution" to stanza three, using "*If* I've" for the number five. Using "sics" for six was interesting, too. I'd never thought of that before, but the form led me to it.

One of our best sestina writers, Marilyn Hacker, insists that sestinas have to be metrical. Her sestina, "From Provence," is written, typically, in iambic pentameter. It begins:

At the Régence, I wonder, is the brain
fed by the eye, or does it feed the eye?
On the red table-top, sunlit, my glass,
half-full, releases fizz into the air . . .

But my poem, "Warpath," like many other sestinas, isn't particularly metrical. There's no patterned meter to it, although some of the lines have similar rhythms. I think the strength of the sestina in general is in its narrative or dramatic thrust. The poet's job is to choose, or discover, six words that for one reason or another make sense being repeated seven times. This obsessive repetition gives the sestina its somewhat aberrant and spooky tone. W. H. Auden uses the words <u>country / vats / wood /</u>

<u>bay / clock / love</u> to scary effect in "Have A Good Time."
Here are the first two stanzas:

> 'We have brought you,' they said, 'a map of the country;
> Here is the line that runs to the vats,
> This patch of green on the left is the wood,
> We've pencilled an arrow to point out the bay.
> No thank you, no tea; why look at the clock.
> Keep it? Of course. It goes with our love.
>
> We shall watch your future and send our love.
> We lived for years, you know, in the country.
> Remember at week-ends to wind up the clock.
> We've wired to our manager at the vats.
> The tides are perfectly safe in the bay,
> But whatever you do don't go to the wood . . .'

Certainly one of the great sestinas is Elizabeth Bishop's much-anthologized "Sestina," in which the words
<u>house /grandmother / child / stove / almanac / tears</u> culmi-
nate in the haunting coda:

> *Time to plant tears*, says the almanac.
> The grandmother sings to the marvelous stove
> and the child draws another inscrutable house.

Auden's and Bishop's lines are roughly tetrameter
(four-beat) but very loose; it's the changes on the repetitions that give the poems their hypnotic force. "My Confessional Sestina," quoted earlier, also isn't consistently
metrical; the lines vary from eight to seventeen syllables.
A major asset of the sestina is that it doesn't necessarily
have to be lyrical like a villanelle or sonnet; it's long
enough to carry different kinds of rhythms within its
stanzas.
   Although when you begin, it's not always easy to see
how your sestina will end, it lends itself to telling stories;

the repeated words help to create and deepen a familiar
landscape (sometimes an internal landscape), as in conversation, in which we tend to say things over and over.
Because of the sestina's narrative capabilities, double
sestinas, like extended conversations, are fairly common.
James Cummins has even written a book, *The Whole
Truth*, which consists of a long sequence of sestinas.

I began the following sestina as a rhymed poem, as
you can tell from the end-words: Bert / skirt / room / then /
dorm / in. After a few drafts, the speaker's obsession with
the girl resulted in repeated words revolving around a
remembered evening as the poem turned into a sestina.
Unlike "Warpath," this begins and ends in iambic pentameter, with lots of exceptions in the middle sections.
The epigraph is from a song from Shakespeare's *As You
Like It*:

Blow, Blow Thou Winter Wind

Then heigh-ho the holly, this life is so jolly!

In my criminal stage I fell in love with Bert
who did an awkward handstand in her skirt
that sent the Sage girls gasping from the room
This was the fifties   life could be shocking then
and I lived like a pig in the college dorm
reserved for Jews and other exiles   Bert moved in

on weekends   A Polish boozer in
love and hate with God   she'd mime His voice: *Bert
hast thou dropped thine pants again?   Thou die!* The
    dorm
hall echoed as she trilled   slipping her skirt
and shoes and jumping on the bed   then
calling for wine or vodka as if my room

were some East Village den   In truth   the room
was smoky   sticky   vile   Sweatshirts festered in

dank mounds   ashtrays stank   She'd flip the stolen
    thin-
stemmed glass over her thin shoulder   Bert
liked to think we had a fireplace   Later we'd skirt
the shards of glass in our bare feet   blow the dorm

and saunter through the snow while half the dorm
hung out their windows   cheering   There wasn't room
for coyness in our act: she'd flap her wet skirt
back at them   take my arm and   heads high in
we'd go   crashing some Christmas party where Bert
would lean on the piano while I cadged drinks   Then

pure as any Shakespearean maid sing *Then
heigh-ho the holly!*   under a lion dorm-
ant on a shield: *Semper liber*   Ah Bert
you were beautiful in those heraldic rooms
your long-lashed umber eyes drowning in
music   And I would clown   sprawled before your skirt

your bare toes tapping out beneath that skirt
their fragile SOS   a neurasthen-
ic code I hopelessly misread   seeing instead only your fine frenzy   If later   in the dorm
you curled weeping in my arms   the room
tight with shadows   I should have whispered   *Bert*

*although this squalid dormitory room
squats in the skirts of hell   your presence here
is holy*   Bert   God loves us now and then

(first published in *The Panhandler*)

The ample room and free rhythms of the sestina enable the writer to work in different tones—conversations,
jokes, quotes, lyrical bursts—as the six words turn in the
wind of the form. Here, I start with a flip conversational
style ("In my criminal stage I fell in love with Bert") that
gradually shifts from external description and humor—
hiding the young woman's desperation under a "party-

girl" facade—to a more formal, almost prophetic tone ("although this squalid dormitory room/squats in the skirts of hell . . .").

A familiar use of this tonal shift can be found in many popular poems, such as Robert Frost's "Mending Wall." Beginning with whimsical chatting and homely images ("I could say 'Elves' to him, / But it's not elves exactly, and I'd rather/He said it for himself"), he shifts tone and rhythm at the end, like a conductor bringing a symphony to its dignified and formal closing: "He moves in darkness, as it seems to me, / Not of woods only and the shade of trees . . ." Note how Frost changes the natural order of the words to slow down the rhythm and thus slow down the reader.

In "Blow, Blow, Thou Winter Wind," I didn't figure this out in advance but followed where the words led me. Once you know you're going to try to write a sestina, you can write out all the end-words, but they are so numerous and so repetitive, it makes you dizzy unless you just go from line to line. I knew, of course, that I wanted to be sympathetic to "Bert" and tell her story, but I didn't know how to do it. The sestina showed me the way, first by suggesting a line from the Shakespearean song—"*Then heigh-ho the holly*" (I was looking for ways to use the end-word "then"). The first line of that song is "Blow, blow, thou winter wind," which became the title and helped set the scene and the tone. So the poem became a contrast between a life that seemed "so jolly" and the cold truth.

In summary: Don't be afraid of the sestina, and don't underestimate it, either. It's not a matter of writing down the end-words and simply filling in; that doesn't work well. All other advice about poetry must be kept in mind. In addition, you have to weave your poem around the six signposts—the end-words—that you've chosen for the journey. The beauty of a poem arises from the intricate relationships of all its parts.

Theodore Roethke, who wrote equally powerful free verse and formal poetry, observed in his *Collected Letters* that form should be thought of "not as a neat mold to be filled, but rather as a sieve to catch certain kinds of material." This is as true for the sestina as it is for the villanelle or sonnet.

To get the feel for how sestinas work, read and reread the sestinas by Ezra Pound, Marilyn Hacker, Dana Gioia, and Anthony Hecht. Soon you'll be spotting them in the works of other poets (John Ashbery, David Evett, Howard Nemerov, Sir Philip Sidney, among others). In any case, when the material for a sestina spirals into your head, your hand should be ready. Try it.

🍃 10

The Pantoum

UNLIKE THE SESTINA, the pantoum is a relatively "new" form in English. Originating from the Malayan *pantun*, the pantoum consists of any number of quatrains from which the second and fourth lines (called *repetons*, because they're repeated) recur as the first and third lines of the next stanza.

The pantoum probably came to us from France (Victor Hugo and Charles Baudelaire used it), but it's hard to find early examples. In fact, the first one I ever read was "Iva's Pantoum" in Marilyn Hacker's collection, *Taking Notice*; but since then it's grown more popular.

The challenge of dealing with a complicated form is one of the pleasures of writing and reading poetry, not unlike playing chess. You can manipulate rules to your advantage, have sudden insights, forward leaps, and reversals. Working with a form like the pantoum tends to become hypnotic ("It haunts you, dawn and evening"), as the repeated lines swim through your mind, looking for a way to hook on grammatically, logically, and emotionally to the previous stanza.

To make the pantoum more complicated (and satisfactory), in the final stanza, lines one and three of the first stanza are reversed, becoming the last line and third-to-last line, respectively; so it begins and ends with the same line. You'll see how this works in the poems that follow.

Some pantoums rhyme, like contemporary poet Vonna Adrian's humorous "A Plaguey Thing," which begins:

> If I were you I'd just forget it:
> A pantoum is a plaguey thing.
> It drives you crazy if you let it;
> It haunts you, dawn and evening.
>
> A pantoum is a plaguey thing.
> My friend, can you define *pantoum*?
> It haunts you, dawn and evening.
> Does it belong in a drawing room? . . .

But most pantoums in English don't rhyme, nor are they humorous. Instead, the repeated lines, like the repeated end-words of the sestina, serve as an excellent substitute for rhyme. The repetition of a word *is* a rhyme, of course, though we usually don't think of a word as rhyming with itself.

To me, most pantoums become more and more intense as the repetition picks up force, almost chant-like in its effect. And because it can be of any length—there are some *long* pantoums!—you never know when it's going to circle back to the beginning, which adds to the suspense. In my "Atomic Pantoum" (next page) I tried to begin with flat, matter-of-fact "scientific" statements that gradually melt into more and more surreal and angry images.

Richard Wilbur has said that one should never sit down to write in a specific form; the very idea is "disgusting." His pronouncement is good advice, generally speaking—but not always.

Of course, the choice of a form should rise out of the material at hand. And yet one can easily imagine Shakespeare sitting down to write a sonnet, or Keats getting ready to write another ode; and if it can be imagined, it can be done. I mention this because when I first learned about the pantoum I remember thinking to myself, "This works just like a chain reaction," and sat down to write "Atomic Pantoum."

Atomic Pantoum

In a chain reaction
the neutrons released
split other nuclei
which release more neutrons

The neutrons released
blow open some others
which release more neutrons
and start this all over

Blow open some others
and choirs will crumble
and start this all over
with eyes burned to ashes

And choirs will crumble
the fish catch on fire
with eyes burned to ashes
in a chain reaction

The fish catch on fire
because the sun's force
in a chain reaction
has blazed in our minds

Because the sun's force
with plutonium trigger
has blazed in our minds
we're dying to use it

With plutonium trigger
curled and tightened
we're dying to use it
torching our enemies

Curled and tightened
blind to the end
torching our enemies
we sing to Jesus

Blind to the end
split up like nuclei
we sing to Jesus
in a chain reaction

(first published in *Poetry*)

Although I had the idea that the pantoum was suitable for and expressive of the subject of a chain reaction, it took me a while to settle on the heavy two-beat (dimeter) lines—the possibility arising because a pantoum line can be of any length:

In a chain reaction
the neutrons released
split other nuclei
which release more neutrons

In "Atomic Pantoum" I liked the drumbeat of the dimeter line, trying to make it stronger as the poem neared the end: "Curled and tightened / blind to the end . . ." In the rewriting, I emphasized the blunt "b" sounds: "blow," "burned," "because," "blazed"; as well as the other sound-related devices: choirs / eyes / fire; plutonium / tightened / torched; fish / fire / force, etc. One of the strengths of the pantoum is that every "device" gets emphasized through repetition (as do awkward phrases as well, so be careful!).
    You'll find that the pantoum pulls you along: When

you've written one stanza, you've already written lines one and three of the next stanza. You have to be especially alert and ready to encourage or discourage various turnings as they emerge ("Two roads diverged in a yellow wood . . ."). To help you keep some control, you can make small adjustments to the repeated lines, to keep them grammatical or to change emphasis. For example, "split other nuclei" becomes "split up like nuclei" in the last stanza. The idea is never to be the prisoner of form but its master, to wrestle with it, to ring changes on it, as in bell ringing, in your own unique voice.

Here's another poem of mine that is a disguised pantoum (a secret code), though when you're familiar with the form, you will recognize it soon enough:

The Secret Code

Bach was rising from another room
like a secret code in a mathematician's castle
when you came toward me in a summer dress
light slatted through the oaken banister
like a secret code in a mathematician's castle
floating down the stairway in the afternoon
light slatted through the oaken banister
an idea of harmony made manifest
floating down the stairway in the afternoon
striping your slender body like a strobe
an idea of harmony made manifest

The music wound you in a golden braid
striping your slender body like a strobe
and Bach and April and undying youth

like music wound you in a golden braid
conspiring until I knew that dream
of Bach and April and undying youth

would cling across the downward years
conspiring until I knew that dream

despite the disharmonic tarnishing of time
would cling across the downward years
and fuse our lives together like a fugue
to spite the disharmonic tarnishing of time

Then all turned mysterious and blessed
and fused our lives together like a fugue
when you came toward me in a summer dress
turning all mysterious and blessed

while Bach was rising from another room

(first published in *The Georgia Review*)

After many tries, I completed this first as a "regular"
pantoum, but then felt that the quatrains didn't help the
meaning. Dividing your poems into stanzas should make
them clearer; if this doesn't happen, rethink the structure. I wanted, if possible, to begin stanzas with "The
music wound you in a golden braid" and "Then all turned
mysterious and blessed," as these seemed like turning
points in the poem.

But I knew I shouldn't simply make random stanzas,
either, in a form as regular as a pantoum—and particularly not in one that features Bach. (I may have been
reading *Godel, Escher, Bach: An Eternal Golden Braid* by
Douglas Hofstadter, which is where the golden braid
came from.)

At any rate, by breaking the poem at those two places,
and with much reworking, I arrived at the symmetrical
"secret code" of 1/4/6/3/3/6/4/1: 28 lines, really seven quatrains, but divided differently (and suitably, because of
the "secret code" theme), which makes the poem more
understandable. Poet/critic Paul Goodman has referred
to "the artistic imperative to make [a poem] as clear as
possible." Note that he said "as possible": Poems can
never be totally explained nor separated from their music
nor reduced to paraphrase.

In "The Secret Code," many lines have small changes in them: switching "and" to "of," "the" to "like," "despite" to "to spite," etc. But the repetitions remain basically complete, and the poem even ends with rhyme—fugue / dress / blessed / room—"more or less" by accident. I also tried to juxtapose certain sounds, made more evident by the repetition of syllables, like "banister" and "manifest," and "disharmonic" and "tarnishing." And many of the words and phrases alliterate: rising / room, code / castle; "harmony made manifest"; "to spite the disharmonic tarnishing of time."

In short, the pantoum is a vibrant form. It's flexible. It can be humorous, narrative, or lyrical. It can be rhymed or not, long or short. But always remember it's a poem first, a pantoum second; otherwise, to quote Goodman again, it will become a "format" instead of a form.

ℬ. 11

The Villanelle

A VILLANELLE is the most difficult of the forms we've been discussing, because it has nineteen lines and uses only two rhymes, a hard assignment in English with its relative paucity of rhyming words, compared to French or Italian, where the form originated. The writer of a villanelle needs to devise septuple (seven!) rhymes.

In addition, rhymed poetry has a tendency to go in and out of favor, so even good villanelles have not always been welcomed by editors. But Welsh poet Dannie Abse was surely right when he wrote in his essay, "On Rhyming and Not Rhyming" (included in his memoir, *A Strong Dose of Myself*), "The fact is, there are no immutable laws of when and where not to use rhyme in poetry or what kind of rhyme is legitimate and acceptable."

The villanelle consists of five tercets, or triplets (three-line stanzas) followed by a quatrain, totaling nineteen lines. (The stanza names you should know are **couplets** (two-line stanzas), **tercets** (three-line stanzas), and **quatrains** (four-line stanzas). The rest are simply numbered, as in six-line stanzas, ten-line stanzas, etc.)

The villanelle uses not only just two rhymes but a set pattern of repeated lines. The first line of the first tercet becomes the last line of the second and fourth tercet; the third line of the first tercet becomes the last line of the third and fifth tercet. Then those same two lines become the last lines of the closing quatrain. Here's an outline to make it clearer, and you'll see it even more clearly in the poem that follows. Let A_1 and A_2 stand for the first and third lines of the first tercet (the capital letters standing for the repeated lines):

lines:

1	A_1
2	b
3	A_2
4	a
5	b
6	A_1
7	a
8	b
9	A_2
10	a
11	b
12	A_1
13	a
14	b
15	A_2
16	a
17	b
18	A_1
19	A_2

The result is an intricate musical pattern that lends itself to many very different effects. In the nineteenth century, W. E. Henley—best known for his poem "Invictus" ("I am the master of my fate; / I am the captain of my soul . . .") —wrote a villanelle, which begins:

A dainty thing's the villanelle;
Sly, musical, a jewel in rhyme,
It serves its purpose passing well.

A double-clappered silver bell
That must be made to clink in chime,
A dainty thing's the villanelle . . .

Henley and fellow Victorian poet Austin Dobson borrowed the form from the French, who got it from the Italians centuries earlier: *Villanella* meant a little rustic song. As the poem above indicates, the villanelle's potential was greatly misread, and for a while it looked as if it would be a dainty or "light" form for limited and pastoral poetry, the way a limerick is limited to humorous verse.

But in the twentieth century, it was taken up and transformed by some of our greatest poets, including Edward Arlington Robinson ("The House on the Hill"), W. H. Auden ("If I Could Tell You"), Theodore Roethke ("The Waking"), Elizabeth Bishop ("One Art") and perhaps especially, Dylan Thomas, whose famous poem, "Do Not Go Gentle Into That Good Night," is as close to a perfect villanelle as one can get.

These poems are ample evidence of the lyrical and dramatic power this form can create. Most villanelles are written in iambic pentameter (as is Thomas's: "Do <u>not</u> go gentle <u>into</u> <u>that</u> good <u>night</u>"), although Robinson's "The House on the Hill" is in short-lined iambic trimeter: "They are <u>all</u> <u>gone</u> <u>away</u>, / The <u>House</u> is <u>shut</u> and <u>still</u>, / There is <u>nothing</u> <u>more</u> to <u>say</u> . . ."

My first book, *The Night Train and the Golden Bird*, concluded with this villanelle:

The Golden Bird

The mind can't sing a poem without the eye
that   staring inward   changes tree to Tree
with roots and branches in the inner sky

The world's a place where real birds really fly
into a distance only children see
The mind can't sing a poem without that eye

The birds disperse   the stormclouds clash on high
while children watch the wild electric tree
that roots and branches in their inner sky

The clouds disperse   the children raise a cry
to see a rainbow curving toward the Tree:
the mind can't sing a poem without that eye

The birds return   the scattered children try
to find the gold that's buried near the Tree
that roots and branches in the inner sky

The clouds return   Children grow old and die
The Tree remains   a golden bird nearby:
the mind can't sing a poem without the eye
whose roots and branches touch the inner sky

(first published in *Inlet*)

This is a poem about the imagination, and how natural it is for children to use it to make symbolic connections (like seeing a jagged lightning bolt as a burning tree in the sky). This "individual" power of imagination often diminishes as we age, but the human imagination itself—the capitalized Tree—is always with us. And hovering around is the golden bird, which may stand for poetry, the arts, the offspring of the imagination, anything that makes our lives deeper and more beautiful.

Note the changes needed to keep the poem reasonably clear and to make a stronger conclusion: adding "touch" in the last line, for instance; changing "with" to "that" and then to "whose." Dylan Thomas and E. A. Robinson make no changes in their repeated lines, but W. H. Auden, Elizabeth Bishop, and Theodore Roethke make numerous and significant ones.

In writing a villanelle, you have to find two interesting lines on which you can create variations, and which will gather power as the poem goes along. "The Golden Bird" became a villanelle, however, only after I realized that I was writing a very organized poem with repetitions: "The birds disperse," "The clouds disperse," "The birds return," "The clouds return." This poem, alas, has at least one obvious weakness. It must be *read* rather than simply *heard*, because it's somewhat dependent on the difference between a *real* tree (small "t"), and the capitalized *imagined* Tree.

The lines in "The Golden Bird" are in the proper villanelle order. In the following poem, though still clearly a villanelle, the order of the first and third lines in subsequent tercets is reversed, thus "straightening them out" in the quatrain. The "idea" for this poem came from a real obsession. I don't know a lot about the logical philosopher Ludwig Wittgenstein, though we studied him briefly in college. Recently I read a poetic novel, *Wittgenstein's Mistress*, by David Markson, and Wittgenstein's dictum, "The world is everything that is the case," returned to me—it's not in the novel—and I couldn't get it out of my head, puzzling it this way and that. I already had been working on a love poem that had the line, "logic lies in poetry's embrace," and one morning I saw that these two fit together. Maybe I tried it as a villanelle because "Wittgenstein," being Austrian, is pronounced "Vittgenstein," and a title came to me: "*Witt*genstein's *Vill*anelle," an alliterative double dactyl! (/— /—). But in the end the title was changed to:

A Meditation on You and Wittgenstein

Wittgenstein never met you face to face
but fancied someone like you when he said
The world is everything that is the case

a maxim hard to fathom   Nevertheless
its rhythms tug like Ariadne's thread:
the world *is* everything that is the case

the world is *everything* that is the case
(you   for example   asleep upon my bed)
Although Wittgenstein never met you face to face

he guessed that logic lies in poetry's embrace
and in the same dark labyrinth has fed
the world being everything that is the case:

for love   or dreams of love   curls at its base
and if you miss it   your heart's bled and dead
I wish he could have met you face to face

An ounce of loneliness outweighs a pound of lace:
What strange equations winding through my head!
Poor Wittgenstein never met you face to face
The world is only   everything: that's the case

I had to reverse the order of the repetition, because
the most important line, the one the speaker is obsessed
with, needs to be repeated immediately, and even an
extra time (in line 7), for the poem to make its best sense.

Once you have settled on the villanelle shape, you
should consider all other poetic elements: alliteration
("logic / lies / labyrinth" leading to "loneliness" and "lace,"
for example); internal rhyme ("bled and dead" matching
up with "face to face" and "Outweighs / lace"); consonance
("maxim / fathom / rhythm"), etc.

That repeated major "line" tugging at me led me to
think of Ariadne, who saved her lover Theseus by giving

him a ball of thread so he could find his way back out of the *labyrinth* (line 11) after hunting down and killing the Minotaur, a monster with the head of a bull and the body of a man. You don't need to know the Greek myth to "understand" the poem, though this would add to your appreciation of it. I like the idea of thinking of love as a dangerous half-human creature (who eats young men and women), curled at the base of the labyrinth of our lives; and knowing the myth helps readers see that. It also supports and darkens the poem as a love poem. The myth of the Minotaur is tragic: Ariadne saves the great hero Theseus, and they go off together; but he later deserts her.

The line, "An ounce of loneliness outweighs a pound of lace" is an example of how form can give you ideas. The line that first came to me, because I was looking for an iambic pentameter line that rhymed with "thread" and "dead," was the old saying, "A pound of feathers equals a pound of lead." Obviously, that wouldn't work, but as I stared at it and tried different combinations, the line I finally used appeared with a different rhyme ("lace"), used in a different place.

One more observation about the villanelle that applies as well to the other forms: Often, as you work on your writing, you'll find a poem approximating a villanelle or a sonnet or even an abecedarian, but refusing, finally, to become one. The rhyme scheme may not work, the repetitions make no sense, the later letters in the alphabet seem inappropriate. In such a case, *pay attention to the poetic idea*, and let the form go where it will.

Many fine poems have resulted from *abandoned* forms, influenced by the form but in the end not a true villanelle or sonnet or whatever. My students have written a number of fine eight-line "sonnets" and abecedarians that stop around the letter "p." One of Paul

Goodman's most famous poems, "The Lordly Hudson"—
actually, the title poem of one of his collections—isn't a
villanelle but couldn't have been written if he hadn't
known what a villanelle was. Here is its first stanza:

"Driver, what stream is it?" I asked, well knowing
it was our lordly Hudson hardly flowing,
"It is our lordly Hudson hardly flowing,"
he said, "under the green-grown cliffs" . . .

The poem goes on with much repetition that creates
the *feeling*, the grace and musicality, of the villanelle
without actually being one.

One of my poems, "Ice," uses the same nineteen-line
rhyme scheme as the villanelle, but skips the repetitions
except for the last line. This poem just wouldn't become a
villanelle, no matter how much I prodded and shuffled it.
It was talky and less rhythmical, closer to the sestina in
its tone. At the same time, the rhymes came along pretty
naturally, and I thought I should keep them. The clincher
came as the poem gathered its religious vocabulary
("blessed, lesson, pulpit, disciples," etc.), and the word
"Gethsemane" (rhyming with "tree") came into my head.
It wasn't going to be exactly a villanelle, but rather like
a "free verse sonnet," it's a direct descendant, showing
once again the flexibility of "fixed" forms:

Ice

The only thing I can remember my father teaching me
is how to carry an ice tray without spilling:
Keep your eye on the front compartment he'd say *you'll see*

it works: not a blessed drop lost Fortunately
that's a practical lesson I've been more than willing
to follow every day of my life so I think of him fondly

as I pad back&forth making ice for our martini
ritual   Mom shrilled from her pulpit *Those are killing*
you   you know   and she was dead-on right   but he

didn't care   nor do we   an inherited suicidal tendency
like a toothpick in the blood   his stoic shrug drilling
into us the appeal of containing your own catastrophe

Peter   he'd smile   holding out his glass   remember
      Gethsemane
was an olive grove   and I'd think of the disciples milling
about   and Jesus waiting for Judas beside an olive tree

and despite my name   as I fixed him his drink with its
      three
olives   I wondered which one was me   in the kitchen
      swilling
gin with my sick old man   waiting for him to say as I
      picked up the tray
Keep your eye on the front compartment: You'll see

(first published in *The Eckerd Review*)

PART THREE: PRACTICALITIES

ℬ. 12

Rewriting

BY NOW, you know that I believe rewriting should be, with occasional lucky exceptions, the major occupation of poets. Poetry is not so much about inspiration as it is about what you do with that original burst of creativity that all poets wait for every day, listening to the world around and inside them, straining to hear what it's saying. Like a call half heard from a distance, poets hear the rhythm, the cadence, some of the words. With practice and patience you can figure it out—almost.

The connection between "world" and "word" is not just semantic; in your poems, both are of equal importance. Poets translate the world into words. If you emphasize the world over the word, you'll have a poem without music to make readers hear; if you emphasize the word over the world, you'll have a poem without a heart to make readers care. A balance between the *world* and the *word* is what poets try to achieve by rewriting.

Poets don't agree on how much rewriting is necessary. Some don't believe in it at all. In the preface to his *Collected Poems*, Allen Ginsberg reiterated his beatnik manifesto: "First thought, best thought. Spontaneous insight—the sequence of thought-forms passing naturally through ordinary mind—was always motif and method of these compositions," though even here "some touches are added and adjustments made."

At an opposite pole would be a poet like Donald Hall, who, in his book *Life Work*, reveals that while he normally rewrites a poem fifty or sixty times, he often rewrites twice that, and on at least one poem, "Another Elegy," he worked through over five hundred drafts. (He counts them, too!)

The question arising from Hall's example, often asked by students, is, "Can we over-rewrite?" That is, can a poet revise so much that the poem's original breath of life gets smothered? The straightforward answer must be Yes, of course it's possible. But I'm convinced that *under*-rewriting is a hundredfold more dangerous than *over*-rewriting, especially for beginning poets. In this aspect of poetry writing, less is not more! Poet/critic John Ciardi said that beginning poets often think they can achieve spontaneity by just letting it spill out on paper, "whereas I find over the years that the impromptu is what begins to happen slowly at the tenth, fifteenth or twentieth draft."

How do you know when a poem's finished? I'm afraid the answer is as simple and irritating as William Butler Yeats's comment, when he said he knew a poem was finished when "something went click" in his head. That's probably right. The task before us as poets is to develop the ability to hear that click.

No substitute exists for wide and deep reading as the preparation for writing. But granting that both Ginsberg and Hall read widely, why does Ginsberg rewrite so little and Hall rewrite so much? I think the poet who rewrites only a little must do a lot of rewriting in his or her head, so that the poem comes out comparatively well-formed. Perhaps also the *kind* of poetry that is closer to improvised jazz needs less rewriting (Jack Kerouac's, for example, or Gregory Corso's).

Formal poetry, oddly enough, seems to help this "spontaneous" process. Byron could sit down and pour out verse after verse in *ottava rima* (eight-line stanzas rhymed abababcc). Merrill Moore could, and did, roll out sonnets like cookies. And at times for every poet, poetry flows out with generosity and ease. But, clearly, most poetry would benefit from serious rewriting (including Ginsberg's, whose *Collected Poems* seems inflated and in need of much cutting: First thought wasn't necessarily best thought). As Ginsberg's friend, and fellow non-rewriter, Kerouac once confessed, "There's a delicate balancing point between bombast and babble." Rewriting will help most poets find that balance.

The young poets I've met who continue to write and publish enjoy rewriting. The amount they rewrite varies a great deal; it depends on how much they can carry in their heads before committing a poem to the page. But written spontaneity is not the same as spoken spontaneity. Some of our most spontaneous-seeming poets (E. E. Cummings and Dylan Thomas come to mind) are, or were, tireless rewriters.

The two major reasons for rewriting are to make the poem *sound better*, and to make the *meaning clearer*. Sound and sense: They can't be separated. Think of how Yeats must have felt when he reached the end of "The Second Coming" and was able to write, "And what rough beast, its hour come round at last, / Slouches towards Bethlehem to be born?" We think, "Powerful and prophetic!" *He* probably thought, "All those great "b" sounds, all that alliteration and assonance!" ("hour," "round," "slouches").

Here's a short poem of which I've preserved most of the early drafts, so that we can walk through it together, seeing the changes as they were made. I often begin a poem in longhand, in a notebook: That's how this one started. I was sitting at our kitchen table describing the scene outside the window.

We were living in Clinton, New York. A winter snowstorm had struck, an occasion of great wonder to a Floridian like me. I was staring out at the buried yard, making little doodles in my notebook, *feeling* as if I were going to have a poem. (I think many writers often feel that way— revved up, bursting with extra alertness, certain that something exciting is about to come along.) I sat there for quite a while; Wordsworth might have said I was communing with nature, readying my soul.

Birds were at the bird feeder, and our cat, Desdemona, was watching them. I wrote down "Dugway Rd." (our address) and "black-capped chickadees & downy woodpeckers, cardinals." Then I looked at the thermometer on the porch wall and began writing the poem. The words in parentheses are crossed out in my notebook:

18 below: the black-capped chickadee
bangs on the suet in front of the cat
pressing against the window: (it seems to me
it's too cold for [illegible])   the woodpile
sprawls disorderly below the porch, (all
is frozen forever in this scene, by these words,
on this page)
                              solid as
The shadow of woodsmoke (while upon) the snow: all
(is) frozen forever in this scene, by these words,
on this page.   A poor farmhouse   broken in by age
And rage, too will never go away:
Your disappointment, bitter as ash, colder / than this
          weather,
is part of what we'd taste like now
if cannibals appeared & cut us up
it never will be better
You're sleeping now: (you never will wake up)

Obviously, this isn't close to being a poem, but the elements of a poem are there. First of all, it surprised me. Here I was, not angry, writing a simple description of a winter scene, and suddenly, triggered I think by the chance rhyme of "age" and "page," a murderous "rage" bursts in, not unlike Browning's "Porphyria's Lover." Also, the short length, spotty rhyme (weather, better), and occasional regular rhythm hinted that this poem might want to be a sonnet.

Poetry needs to be localized, to have specific images that evoke both recognition and emotion. All of this poem's imagery, though simple, suggested death and violence: the snow, the bitter cold, the chickadee (a common bird, but black-capped like an executioner, and "banging" on suet, or dead animal fat), the cat wanting to get at the bird (actually many birds, but the poem isolates one), the fire. Everything can be taken at least two ways. Before long, a merely picturesque scene began to suggest a world in uproar, like Tennyson's "Nature, red in tooth and claw."

Now with different eyes, I looked more closely at the yard. I noticed the dark surrounding woods, and the stump (more violence) of what used to be a huge elm tree, and I added these to the poem. I also knew, from the moment I wrote it, that the line about cannibals was ludicrous and embarrassing and would have to go. But I wrote it down because it popped into my head—no censorship on first drafts! —and its note of fear and threat was right. This "first thought" was helpful in discovering what the poem would be about, but like the first soldiers up a hill, its life would be short.

I worked through many drafts, making small changes at a time, typing and retyping it, calling it first "The Farmer," then "January," and finally "Rage." I dropped "disorderly" because "sprawls" implies it. I changed "win-

dow" to "pane," which both sounds better and is a homo-
phone for "pain." I added the line ending with
"emptiness," making it a short line with a patch of empty
space after it.

After I made "sense" of the story, ambiguous as it is,
I began working on the sound. First I emphasized the
"forever," "never," "weather," "better" progression by
making them end-words, and added alliteration ("more /
murderous," "now . . . never," etc. I tried to make a sonnet, but never quite got there, unless you want to call
it a free verse sonnet, which is perhaps an oxymoron.
It wound up being a fourteen-line poem broken into a
sonnet-like octet and sestet, with some rhyme and a
rhythm suggesting iambic pentameter:

Rage

Eighteen below: the black-capped chickadee
bangs on the suet in front of the cat
pressing against the pane   The woodpile
sprawls below the porch   the woodsmoke shadow
solid as the snow   the emptiness
where the old elm used to be: all frozen forever
in this scene   by these words   on this page:
a poor farmhouse broken down by age

And rage   too   will never go away   never
Your disappointment   bitter as ash   more
murderous than this weather
is part of what we'd taste like now
if whatever's in the woods got in the house
You're sleeping now: you never had it better

(first published in *The New Yorker*)

This summary of the process of writing this poem
leaves out various wrong turnings, extra lines and images that came and went. A deer emerged from the woods

while I was working on the poem, my gloves burned up
because I left them on the pipe leading from the wood
stove—but these details only confused the poem, so I
omitted them. I tried it in the past tense, but as usual
with poetry, the present tense was stronger, more immediate in its impact. Finally, when I had made it as
straightforward as I could, when every line had only
what was necessary, when I decided on "You're sleeping
now: you never had it better" (which by now sounded like
"bitter" to me), I called it quits. It's possible that a poem
is never completed, only abandoned, but the poet should
stay in his or her poem until the very last instant, before
leaping to another.

Here's another example from my notebook. We often
go to the Olive Garden restaurant, and one time we had
a long wait. I studied the people around us, listened to
the piped-in classical music; and made some notes in my
pocket notebook, including the first sentence, a play on
Wordsworth's "I Wandered Lonely as a Cloud." A pretty
woman in the group had an extraordinarily sad expression (though of course I could have been misreading it). I
thought about her during the evening, and the next
morning the poem came out, almost "finished," like this:

We were waiting lonely in a crowd to be seated
at the Olive Garden   A momentary silence
and the heavy strings of background music swept
forward like a storm sweeping across a prairie
soaking the twelve of us so that
a woman in a red hat suddenly burst into tears
small shoulders shaking   earrings bouncing the
    ceiling
light across the plastic grapes surrounding posters of
    Rome
& Florence   We stared at her while the violins
went crazy and I knew / one hundred years ago
some Italian composer in a small room in Siena

wrote this piece for this exact moment when what he
    felt
would be felt by someone else in precise proportions of
grief and relief   a stricken friend locked in his own
    head
a lovely child gone wrong   a father distant as the moon
and everyone in the waiting room / understood this
    clearly
as if receiving these messages in a (legato) trance
drawing together from every race & class as if
we could get along   given half a chance
and though the waiters happily didn't sing
and the manager maintained a dubious dignity
and no one exactly bared his or her soul
the computer salesman in front of us held out his hand
and the woman took it and stood up and they danced
just a few steps   but they danced   before some table
    cleared
& we moved on to pasta & fageoli

Several ideas are circulating in this poem. I had to do
at least three things: *recognize* what it was about; *organize* it to make it clearer; and *harmonize* the sound with
its sense. Because the original impulse was somehow
connected to Wordsworth's poem, I reread "I Wandered
Lonely as a Cloud." It's about how the beauty of the
"crowd" of "golden daffodils" remains with us forever,
preserved by "that inward eye / Which is the bliss of solitude." In my poem, the woman takes the place of the daffodils (and it's true that I can still see her today). But two
other elements are here, as well: *art*—the Italian composer—and the *effect* of art on the mixed audience and,
by extension, society.

    The poem seemed to fall roughly into three equal
parts—the Woman, the Music, and the Group—so as I
rewrote the original 26 lines in this way, I gradually divided it into three nine-line stanzas (adding a line).
Wordsworth's dancing daffodils perhaps suggested the

dance at the end; I know that after many drafts I added "the inward eye" and took the word "pensive" from Wordsworth's poem, substituting it for the manager's "dubious" dignity.

I thought the poem needed a long first sentence to match the long wait and pull the reader into the room with the music, so the first eight lines became one sentence, smoothed by alliteration ("storm" and "stand," "shoulders shuddering," etc.) and other related sounds. "Twelve" became "nine" to go with "pines," which made a more visually sensible substitution for "prairie."

These many changes were not thought out in this neat way, of course, but appeared piece by piece as I said the lines to myself and shaped the poem the way a potter shapes his clay.

When you read the final version you can see the changes for yourself. I think the woman's sad expression triggered my own painful memories, which are often a primary source of poetry. I also wanted to say something meaningful and specific about the power of art in our lives, but without sentimentalizing or exaggerating it. I'm convinced, for example, that poetry *is* powerful, though its effects on readers are variable and hard to measure precisely.

The Olive Garden

We were waiting lonely in a crowd to be seated
at the Olive Garden   when a momentary silence sucked
the heavy strings of background music forward
like a storm across a stand of pines
shaking the nine of us so that a woman in a green hat
suddenly began to cry   small shoulders shuddering
earrings bouncing the ceiling light over plastic grapes
clustered on posters of Naples and Rome   We stared
at her while violins called her name   and I knew

a hundred years ago some strung-out stranger
in a rented room in Siena wrote this piece
for this exact moment when what he felt
would be felt by someone else in precise proportions
of grief and relief   the inward eye seeing a stricken friend
locked in his own head   a lovely child gone wrong   a
     father
remote as Mars: everyone in the reception room
understanding this clearly   messages absorbed
poco a poco   in a rhythmic trance   drawing us

together from every race and class as if we could get
along given half a chance   and though the waiters happily
didn't sing and the manager maintained a pensive dignity
and no one exactly bared his or her soul
the computer salesman next to us put down
his briefcase and held out his hand
so the woman took it and stood up and they danced
just a few steps   before the tables cleared
and we moved on to *pasta e fagiol'*

(first published in *The Tampa Review*)

From this account of the process I used, I hope you
can understand the reasons behind the various changes,
possibly most clearly by looking at the proper names. In
the original first stanza, I had written "Florence," from
my notes. The substitution of "Naples" goes better with
"grapes" and leads to "name" on the next line. I changed
"small" to "rented" to go better with "Siena," leading to
"felt" and "else." And I could have written "a father remote as Pluto," but instead chose "Mars" for its related
sounds, as well as the implication of a military sternness.

I also wanted to use some Italian—the Olive Garden
is an Italian restaurant and I was imagining an Italian
composer—so I chose *poco a poco* (a musical direction
meaning "little by little"), thinking it was appropriate
used with "rhythmic." Then I ended the poem on *pasta e
fagiol'* from the menu, dropping the final "i" as is done in

speech, making a rhyme (though separated by five lines) with "soul."

This is free verse, so there are no set rules for how long each line should be or what the end-words should be. Each line should have its own dynamic, its own energy, fitting into the rest of the poem like a piece in a puzzle. I decided on ending the first two stanzas with "I knew" and "drawing us," respectively, because the two phrases create tension (knew what? drawing us where?) and then open up to a new thought.

One way to approach rewriting is to draw a line under *every* "soft spot," i.e., every word or phrase you have a doubt about or think isn't necessary or strong enough, for whatever reason. Remember, poetry is the art of compression. It should be hard and clean, with *no* soft spots. Then begin with those changes, and that will invariably lead to others.

It also helps to allow time to elapse between rewritings. Let the poem cool off a bit, so you can handle it more easily. Never send a poem out until at least six months after you've first written it. Most of the time, you will have improved your poem during those months.

In short, there isn't one way to rewrite a poem, or an optimum number of rewritings to work through. But in general you should 1) study your poem to see what it's trying to say, 2) shape the poem to clarify that intention, and 3) work on the sound until it all comes together to your complete—or almost complete—satisfaction.

ℬ. 13

Necessary Reading

MY SUGGESTED reading for beginning (or advanced) poets can be interpreted differently by each individual poet. You can't read too much, *but* don't put off your writing to read. Writing first, reading second. There's no end to the reading you can do.

What to read? The great poets beginning with Chaucer (or earlier, with "Beowulf"). The Modernists, especially Yeats, Eliot, Pound, Stevens, Moore, Williams. Post-1950 English and American poets, notably Philip Larkin, Robert Lowell, Elizabeth Bishop, Theodore Roethke, Muriel Rukeyser. Contemporary poets like Stanley Kunitz, Alicia Ostriker, Robert Pinsky, Thomas Lux, Richard Wilbur, Maxine Kumin, William Jay Smith, Susan Ludvigson, Edward Field, Ted Kooser, Molly Peacock, Charles Wright, William Meredith, Mark Strand, Paul Zimmer, Rita Dove, and Dionisio Martınez make a good start.

You don't have to read these poets in any particular order. In general, novice poets should begin with contemporary poetry, to get the idea of what's being written now. These poets will speak to you most directly and then lead you back through literary history. You could, for example, read a young poet who was influenced by Howard Nemerov, who was influenced by Yeats and Frost, who were influenced by Pound and Wordsworth, who were influenced by Chinese poetry and Milton, *ad infinitum*. These connections are abundantly discussed in most anthologies, as well as in reviews, articles, and essays in magazines and literary journals.

Eventually, of course, it would be worthwhile (and enjoyable) to become familiar with the history of English and American poetry, to identify the Cavalier poets, the Metaphysical and Neoclassical poets, the Romantics, the Victorians, right up through the Beatniks, the New York School, the Language poets, and the New Formalists. In the lives of poets, biography after biography tells us: If you're interested in poetry, you'll be interested in all of it. (Well, almost all.) But I wouldn't pursue these poets as required reading. So much that you'll love is out there, you should just wander like a tourist from flower to flower, from garden to garden, and from field to field; one day you'll check your passport, and it will say: Poet.

Foreign poetry in translation is also important, or, if you're fluent in another language, read it in the original. French poetry (Baudelaire, Rimbaud, Verlaine, Laforgue) influenced the Modernists; Spanish-speaking poets (Neruda, Paz, Aleixandre) have been very influential on American poets since 1950. I know some French poetry by heart, but mainly I read foreign poets in translation. You might start with the Nobel Prize-winners, because they're more readily available, and go on from there. The wonderful poems of Polish poets Czeslaw Milosz (1980) and Wislawa Szymborska (1996) are in most libraries and bookstores, as are those of Pablo Neruda (Chilean, 1971), Eugenio Montale (Italian, 1975), Vicente Aleixandre (Spanish, 1977), Odysseas Elytis (Greek, 1979), Jaroslav Seifert (Czechoslovakian, 1984), Joseph Brodsky (Russian-American, 1987), and Octavio Paz (Mexican,

1990). (The dates indicate the year they were named Laureates.)

Though of course these volumes of poetry are available in good public and college libraries, nothing can replace *owning* them so you can pick them up whenever you wish, make notes in them, and carry them from place to place like lucky charms. If you want to write poems, eventually you should have your own poetry library, reflecting your tastes and enthusiasms. Go to your local bookstore frequently, browse for an hour or so, and pick out a book of poems on each visit. This may encourage your bookseller to carry more volumes of poetry, and it will enrich you forever.

One of the best ways to find out what you like is to read the magazines that publish poetry. The "slick" magazines publish a few poems, and it's always interesting (and often irritating) to see what they're publishing. But there are dozens, probably hundreds, of lively literary magazines, beginning with the old established ones like *Poetry, The Hudson Review, The Sewanee Review,* and *The Paris Review.* The ones I like best—though I'm always trying new ones and my list changes constantly— are *The Georgia Review, Tampa Review, Shenandoah, The Virginia Review,* and *The Gettysburg Review.* You can find a selection of these journals in a good library. It's also a good idea to subscribe to a few each year, and then switch around; in this way you'll come to know what kind of poetry the editors publish, and whether your own work might fit into that group. *The Directory of Poetry Publishers* (Dustbooks) is very helpful in making your selection.

For information about what's going on in the "literary world," i.e., conferences, writing colonies, contests and awards, interviews, debates, calls for submission, etc., the two invaluable "professional" publications are *Poets & Writers* and *The Writer's Chronicle.* These are very handy, up-to-date, and will tell you what you need to know about workshops, trends in the marketplace, new and small presses, and the like. A somewhat broader net is cast by writers' magazines like *The Writer*, which is geared for beginning and amateur writers as well as the more advanced.

Around your work area you'll need some reference books for handy access. On my desk I have *Webster's Collegiate Dictionary*, *Roget's International Thesaurus*, *The Columbia Viking Desk Encyclopedia*, and *Bartlett's Dictionary of Quotations*.

The dictionary is the most important, and besides a decent one you'll need for spelling and basic definitions, you should have access to the *Oxford English Dictionary (OED)*, probably the two-volume Compact Edition with its magnifying glass. The unabridged *OED* is available in most college libraries. This is enormously useful to a writer. For example, take a word like "glossary." *Webster's* simply shows how to spell and pronounce it, and says "a collection of textual glosses or of specialized terms with their meanings." But the *OED* tells us its derivations from the Latin "glossarium" and the French "glossaire," and, after defining it more fully than the *Webster's*, gives many wonderful examples of its early use, beginning with Caxton in 1483 ("it is said in the glosarye that . . ." etc.) up to an 1838 quote from Dickens in *Nicholas Nickleby*: "The expression on a man's face is commonly a help to his thoughts, or glossary on his speech." The *OED* goes on to give much more information about the word, and as such is invaluable in the making of poems, where each word is weighed.

Over the years, I've often "asked for" different reference books as gifts, so in my personal library I have such works as *The Encyclopedia of Poetry and Poetics*, Clement Wood's *Rhyming Dictionary*, *The Encyclopedia of*

North American Birds, a *Zip Code Directory*, *The Rand McNally World Atlas*, lots of art books, *The Oxford Annotated Bible*, *The Larousse Encyclopedia of Mythology*, *The Oxford Dictionary of English Etymology*, *The Oxford Anthology of English Literature*, *Chambers's Technical Dictionary*, various editions of *The Writer's Handbook*, and an assortment of French, Italian, Polish, German and other foreign language dictionaries. My office and house are cluttered with poetry and fiction, magazines and anthologies, the typical accumulation of a lifetime spent around books. The floor-to-ceiling bookshelves that cover one wall in my house are lovelier than any wallpaper could ever hope to be.

Because of the size of my poetry collection, I've found it helpful to more or less alphabeticize it by author. Otherwise, it can take forever to find a book or a poem that I need at a given moment.

❦ 14

Practical Advice

IN MANY WAYS, practicality and poetry-writing are worlds apart. *You're not going to get rich or famous writing poetry.* Stop any person randomly, and ask him or her to name three contemporary poets: You will get a blank stare. But poetry writing, like virtue, is its own reward.

Poets live in the real world where they have to make a living, raise families, find time to write, know where to send their work, etc. So in this chapter I'll briefly discuss jobs, workshops, conferences, contests, and publishing in general.

1) *Jobs*: Some poets, like James Merrill and Robinson Jeffers, are born wealthy or inherit a livable income, but most have to figure out how to survive and write poetry at the same time. "Money," said Wallace Stevens, "is a kind of poetry." I'm not sure what that means—it's necessary for life, maybe—but like everyone else, poets have to be concerned about money.

Poets have been farmers (Robert Frost and Wendell Berry); doctors (William Carlos Williams and Dannie Abse); editors (Grace Schulman and Stanley Kunitz); insurance executives (Wallace Stevens and Ted Kooser);

businessmen (Dana Gioia and Richard Eberhart); advertising directors (James Dickey and Robert Phillips); lawyers (Edgar Lee Masters and Lawrence Joseph); priests (Gerard Manley Hopkins and Daniel Berrigan); librarians (Marianne Moore and Philip Larkin); diplomats (Archibald MacLeish and Pablo Neruda); and art curators (Frank O'Hara and John Ashbery). T.S. Eliot took great pride in getting promoted while he was a banker. Walt Whitman reviewed his own poetry (favorably) while working as a newspaper reporter. Poets have been housewives and househusbands, factory workers and military men and women. Essentially, any job that you can handle, that supports you, and leaves some time and energy left over for poetry, is fine.

But poets are always looking for *more time*, so it's no accident that most writers today teach at colleges and universities. Many say that there are three reasons for this attachment: June, July, and August. And it's true that in most cases, especially at universities, writers have more time to write than they would at different occupations.

In addition, teaching college students brings you into contact with youthful energy, contemporary vocabulary, new music, fresh attitudes. You spend lots of time in libraries, with easy access to all its magazines and newspapers, as well as books. And you're surrounded by people who think literature is important, and who enjoy talking about it. If you enjoy working with students, this is the right life for you.

(Teaching in primary and secondary schools is harder for a writer. I've done both and can testify that after a day of teaching eighth graders, say—and probably coaching a team and advising the yearbook and monitoring lunch period—there's little time or energy left over after you've finished grading your papers. Grade school and high school teachers are often saints, but they're seldom practicing writers—though I know of some admirable exceptions.)

There are two main drawbacks to teaching: 1) For some, it depletes the very kind of creative energy they need for their writing; and 2) many others feel that *because* most writers today are teachers, with everyone having similar experiences, it would be advantageous to do something different. This is partially true. On the other hand, teachers undergo the same passions, betrayals, losses, ecstasies, hopes and ambitions as anyone else, in any line of work; not only that, I've known teachers to undertake the most amazing adventures in their free months: canoeing down the Amazon, sailing in the Aegean, living with Palestinians in Jerusalem, buying a broken-down chalet in southern France. Most teachers, in short, have no problem with finding something "different" to write about.

If possible, beginning poets should do whatever work they enjoy, or whatever work leaves them the most free time and energy. *If* you decide to join the majority and go into college teaching, I also think you should get the highest degree available, not just to make your job safer and more permanent, but to make you more knowledgeable in your field.

2) *Workshops*: Young people interested in writing naturally gravitate, and are guided, toward writing workshops—though nowadays these are not necessarily academic, and are often sponsored by various community organizations.

Workshops are helpful to most young or beginning writers. Some writers don't like talking about their work, don't want to change it, or hear criticism about it, but they do want to hear what other people think about their writing, and workshops are where this happens.

Workshops have been accused of turning out second-rate poets, pale imitations of their teachers. But even when this is true, it's beside the point. *Most* poetry isn't first-rate, and *most* writers begin by imitating other writers whom they admire. *A workshop is only a stepping-stone, not a destination.*

In my experience, serious young—and not-so-young— poets have markedly improved their work through workshops. In fact, the poems that have come through my classes have constantly surprised me by their variety, energy, and originality. This is not to say I've never held my head in despair:

Teaching Poetry in a Country School in Florida

It ain't there   Come off it   Rousseau
The eyes roll inward   the brain coughs
like a motor at ten below

and doesn't start: they're not bad kids
Too dumb for poetry   and smart enough to know
they don't need it: no one needs it:
not their teachers   nor principal   nor coach
who equates it with queers
and public masturbation
which unfortunately it sometimes resembles
particularly the iambic

But we have to do it because
in the midst of that tangible boredom
from that stack of pathetic papers
there is always one you come across
just before turning to drink
with thought of murder or suicide
there is always one who writes
My wings are invisible but brilliant:

they carry me to the dark forest
where the unicorns kneel in prayer . . .

So   You go on   after a while
But still   all that effort   so little to show
like that royal palm outside my window going up & up
and up   with a small green *poof* at the top
(first published in *The New Republic*)

Writers can save a lot of time, avoid a lot of mistakes, by taking a workshop; they can find out what poets and poetry to read, get an idea of standards and styles, identify writing tics that had been unnoticed, and, perhaps most important of all, meet some friends to help make the literary life a reality and an ongoing engagement. Workshops are sometimes invigorating even to established writers who have written for a long time: It's like meeting someone fresh and talented in a coffee house or cafe: Your life takes on renewed interest and energy.

In a famous anecdote about Flannery O'Connor, herself the product of the mother of all writing workshops, the University of Iowa, O'Connor was asked if she thought workshops stifled young writers. "If you ask me, they don't stifle enough of them," she's supposed to have replied. That's funny and cruel, like her stories, but aspiring writers are going to follow her example and not her epigrams, and continue to fill the nation's expanding program of workshops. I think this is the right thing for them to do.

3) *Conferences*: For many of the same reasons, I think conferences are often worthwhile, maybe because they're usually fun. Most writing magazines, like *The Writer*, will list conferences in your area, though I know some writers who use writing conferences as a way to see different parts of the country. You might go because you want to

hear John Updike, Alicia Ostriker, Fred Chappell, or Nikki Giovanni, to name a few who frequently appear. Just hearing such writers talk and read—and perhaps chatting with them, getting a signed copy of their books—is worthwhile in itself.

You might prefer conferences that offer a close reading and criticism of your manuscript by published writers. Others feature influential editors and agents; some have lots of poetry readings. Conferences can last a day or two weeks, be expensive or cheap, very large or quite small: You have to get information and choose the right conference for you.

If you don't expect too much from either workshops or conferences, they can be worthwhile and pleasant experiences—sometimes extremely so. No one but you is going to make you a writer, but in these settings you can find encouragement, advice, and, if you're lucky, friendship, inspiration, and the occasional useful contact.

4) *Contests*: Contests, too, can serve a useful purpose, if you don't feel that winning or losing one will change your life. I'm in favor of legitimate contests and have judged a fair number of them. Writing poetry doesn't usually bring recognition or tangible awards, and contests go a little way to rectify that. Sometimes they can give you the hope and momentum you need to continue, though to tell the truth, if you're a real writer, you'll continue anyway, without much encouragement.

Perhaps the best reason to enter contests is that they make you look at your own work critically, to pick out the "best" poem, or group of poems, to submit; or if it's a contest for book-length manuscripts, it provides the impetus for you to put the poems in a meaningful order. A contest often serves as a prod for you to get your work up to snuff, to get it typed up neatly and correctly—professionally—ready to be read by a critical editor and judge.

Enter legitimate contests, if you're so inclined. Give them your best shot and then forget about them, until the winners are announced. Most contests—like lotteries—are extraordinarily hard to win. Luck is a large component, and this should be remembered whether you win or lose. If you have any doubt about the legitimacy of the contest—some just take the fee, publish all entries, and try to get you to buy an expensive and wretched book—check with someone who knows. You can usually find out by calling the Creative Writing department of the nearest college.

Contests can add a little spice to your life and get you, when you're ready, to send those poems, dressed in their very best, out in the world; and after all, that's the reason you're writing. Just remember, you're not a failure when your poem doesn't win, and you're not Robert Frost or Emily Dickinson when it does. You're a writer—which is an honorable occupation—who has been lucky or unlucky in this particular contest.

5) *Publication*: Almost all writers want to publish what they've written. Unfortunately, many poets want to publish before their poems are ready. One of the ways a workshop can be useful is to help poets recognize that a particular poem isn't ready; there's still work to be done on it. Of course, in the end, the decision of whether or not to send out a poem for publication is yours, but my rule would be, *Better late than early*. Poetry isn't breaking news, but "news that stays news." Take your time.

When you're ready to send out your work, the most practical move is to find out what publications are in your area, *and read these magazines*. They're the ones in which your work has the best chance of being accepted, as magazines are often eager to find local talent.

Remember that most of these publications are national in their scope and ambition, so the competition is as fierce as elsewhere; but if you're from the area, the editors would naturally be interested in looking at what you've done.

After you get a few acceptances, try to widen your circle. Go to the library or bookstore and read a few of the current literary journals, *The Hudson Review*, perhaps, or *The Sewanee Review*. Check the national magazines like *The Nation, The New Republic, The Atlantic*. Even though the chances of acceptance here are minuscule, statistically speaking, every year they publish some new writers. Here's old advice, but helpful: It's best to read what these magazines publish, to get an idea whether your own poetry might appeal to the editors.

I began publishing in small midwestern magazines. Many are long defunct (the life of most literary magazines is short), but some, like *The Carleton Miscellany* and *The Antioch Review*, are ongoing and distinguished. The first "national" magazine my poems appeared in was *The New Republic* and for many years I published there, while Reed Whittemore and then Doris Grumbach were the poetry editors. Magazines change with their editors, and writers go in and out of favor. You can't control this; all you can do is keep your work circulating.

After you've published in a fair number of magazines, it would be natural for you to try to publish a chapbook. Most chapbooks—again, you should do some research— are handsomely done, in small print runs of two to five hundred. Your poems may not reach many people, but publishing a chapbook is generally a very satisfactory and worthwhile experience. (In addition, many chapbook publishers sponsor contests.)

The last, and most important, step is the book. Although more universities publish poetry now, it's still very difficult to publish a book. But if you're a poet, this is what you have to try to do—*when* your poems are ready. Trying to win a contest is one way to do it. *Poets & Writers* will show you that there are a large number of contests nowadays, though your chances remain small. Still, each year, a few new writers win them. Now, of course, with the prevalence of copying machines, you can enter several contests and send your manuscript to several publishers at the same time.

So, the usual path of a published poet goes something like this: college literary magazines, local magazines and newspapers, regional and national magazines and journals, a chapbook, and then a book-length collection. Many poets skip one or more of these steps, but this would be a natural progression. And some great poets— Emily Dickinson is the most famous example—don't get to the last step in their lifetimes.

But of course it's *not* the last step. When you finally have a book accepted, how does your life change? You have a book to hold in your hand, and this is satisfying— but what do you actually do? You do the same thing you've always done: Sit down and write more poetry, and then send it out. Beginning and published poets are doing exactly the same thing, and the last step is always your next poem.

You shouldn't judge yourself by your publications, but by your best work, always trying to make yourself a better poet and a better judge of your own and others' poetry. Perhaps you shouldn't judge yourself at all. Writers write; judges judge.

ℬ. 15

Why Write Poetry?

Not yesterday I learned to know
  The love of bare November days
Before the coming of the snow,
But it were vain to tell her so,
  And they are better for her praise.

(from "My November Guest," by Robert Frost)

IN A DESPONDENT, self-doubting mood (a mood well-known to poets), the fine American poet and editor Theodore Weiss once said to Dannie Abse, "Unless you're hailed as among the first of your generation—unless you're famous in the way that Lowell is or Berryman is—is it worth the game?" And Abse answered, "Well, there's no choice, Ted."

Yes, writers are going to write, no matter what. But I would go further than that: At all levels, writing is "worth the game." To have poetry woven into the fabric of your lives, reading it and writing it, is a rich privilege. The very act of writing poetry deepens your recognition that the universe is connected, your life has depth, and your relationship with the world has meaning. Whether your poems "succeed" or "fail" is secondary to your involvement in this difficult but necessary quest to write something beautiful.

This book is aimed at beginning writers—speaking broadly—of whatever age, though I hope, too, it holds some interest for those more advanced. The writer of "how-to" books can't avoid sounding like the old and fatuous Polonius advising the young and mercurial Laertes: "This above all: to thine own self be true, / And it must follow, as the night the day, / Thou canst not then be false to any man." So be it. But remember, much of Polonius's advice is excellent.

Why Polonius sounds ridiculous (as compared, say, to Hamlet) is, I believe, not that he's wrong, but that he lacks anguish. He's the foil for the tormented *poetic* soul of Hamlet: "How weary, stale, flat, and unprofitable / Seem to me all the uses of this world." Hamlet is the perfect model of a poet.

Similarly, it's harder to write happy poems than sad or tragic poems. You seem like a dog wagging its tail while all around you people are starving, marriages are crashing, politicians are lying, entire countries are disintegrating, and injustice is rampant. But Despair is only part of the human story, the evil twin of Hope. And poetry, even at its darkest, is on the side of Hope. In Dream Song #29, where John Berryman is lamenting the death of his friends ("The high ones die, die. They die. You look up and who's there?"), he inserts this observation: "This is not for tears; / thinking."

Much sadness runs through the *Dream Songs*, as it did in Berryman's life, but the poems themselves are high-spirited, conveying a sense of the value and beauty and mystery of our world. We write poetry to sing this world, with all its warts and sinkholes.

My colleague at Eckerd College, the novelist Sterling Watson, often gives this advice to his students: *Quit if you can.* This is not so much a directive as a description. If you have a calling to write, you're going to write, and no amount of discouragement can derail you. But this doesn't mean you won't need help and encouragement, which is what this book is for.

As a poet, you need to hold these contradictory truths in your head: You're alone and no one can do this but you; and at the same time, you're part of a living tradition going back to Chaucer and Wordsworth and Dickinson and Frost, including all those, like you, writing today and all those readers still to come.

The typical progress of a poem goes something like this: You work on it—from conception to writing to rewriting—for a few months, and then maybe you wait a few months more to make sure it's "finished." Then you send it out to a small magazine, which sits on it for six months before sending it back, with or without a note. So you take a deep breath, retype it, and send it out again. After another six months (if you're lucky), you get a good letter from an editor. They love your poem and want to publish it. A year later your poem comes out, and you receive your three copies of *The Grape Leaf Review*— circulation unknown but minuscule—from somewhere in North Dakota. By this time you're deep into other poems, and barely remember this one. Delayed gratification is more complicated than you may have thought.

I tried to get a quicker and more direct response with this poem:

Dear Reader

Why don't you write you never
write   each day I check the mail
nothing but truss ads & christmas seals
where are you what are you doing
tonight?

How are your teeth?
When I brush mine blood

drips down my chin
are you happy do you miss me
I will tell you
there is no one like you
your eyes are unbelievable
your secrets are more interesting than anyone else's
you had an unhappy childhood
right?

I will rub your feet they're tired
I'll say Hey
let's go to the movies
just the 2 of us
love

peter

                    (first published in *The New Republic*)

I *did* get some wonderful and funny letters in reply.
Readers of poetry *are* out there. But not many noticed
that the poem is divided symmetrically into stanzas of 5/
10/5, and that the title and my name at the end rhyme,
etc. Writers attack loneliness technically, looking for the
music locked in our everyday language, waiting to be
freed:

Dear Reader . . .
lets go to the movies
just   the twoofus
love . . .
peter

Why write poetry? Why breathe? Wallace Stevens's
lines in "Sunday Morning" come to mind: "We live in an
old chaos of the sun / . . . / Or island solitude, unsponsored,
free." Our lives *do* seem chaotic, one aspect unrelated to
the next: ourselves, nature, work, society, governments,
history, the future. Where's the connection? Octavio Paz

has said that poetry is the antidote to technology and the market, because it builds and strengthens our imagination, the only human faculty that can make these connective leaps.

Reasons for writing poetry are as numerous as individual writers: because we're lonely, to impress a boyfriend, to thank someone, to make money, because we're happy. But I believe there are four main reasons:

1) *We want to discover what we think.* The great French poet Paul Valery claimed that the only reason he wrote was to study the way his own mind worked (*"Mes vers ont ete surtout pour moi des exercices"*). Plunging deep into our own subconscious, we often come up with thoughts, beliefs, memories that we didn't know were there. Poetry, as a voyage of self-discovery, is an important part of the trip. "How can I know what I think till I see what I say?" is a funny old question. It's typical of a poet to be surprised at his or her poems—in fact, it's probably necessary: As Frost said, "No surprise in the writer, no surprise in the reader."

2) *We have to.* "Writer's block" is a normal part of any poet's life, but we learn over the years that this is a time when the well of feeling and ideas is filling up again, and is part of the normal cycle. Some poets don't seem to suffer from writer's block—the prolific Lyn Lifshin and Joyce Carol Oates are examples—but most go at least from periods of high productivity to low. In all writers, the urge to write always returns, only sharpened by inactivity.

Some poets feel they have to travel, experience adventures and tangled liasons in order to write, but this isn't true. These experiences can be part of life, but aren't necessary for poetry. Rilke pointed out to his young correspondent, "That which we call destiny goes forth from *within* people, not from without into them" (my italics). What one should do "between" poems is simple: Study. Read the poets you haven't read. Reread the great poets. Read philosophy. Listen to music. Relax and play some tennis. Hold yourself open to what's around you, especially new thoughts and new ideas. To quote Valery again, "In the poet / the ear speaks, / the mouth listens . . ."

3) *We believe life has meaning, however defined.* Psychologists tell us that the brain is constantly searching for relationships, and part of the satisfaction of poetry is that it's involved in that search. This ultimately involves the search for truth, and poets often bring forth ideas that are unfashionable, politically incorrect, even subversive. (I remember vividly the excitement, and the anger, in Minneapolis when back in the early sixties, Robert Bly organized readings by "Poets Against the Vietnam War," before that attitude was widespread.) In politically repressed countries, poets are often the first to get censored, as the lives of Osip Mandelstam, Anna Akhmatova, Stansilaw Baranczak and Czeslaw Milosz, among others, testify. Because our first concern is with language, rather than with doctrine, even apolitical writers will be suspect. What did he or she mean by that? The attempt to say something true and beautiful can lead you into uncharted waters.

Here are the last two stanzas of a poem of mine called "Multiple Readings for National Poetry Month":

. . .
Where was I? . . . I think the women are right: if food
and sex are all that matters   a dog's life   upbeat
and flatulent   would be better than ours   But dogs
are neither disturbed nor soothed by verbal magic:
And the white breast of the dim sea

And all dishevelled wandering stars . . . Across our
audience hope and grace bloom like peonies
after summer rain   heads nodding with intricate

incandescence   our poem a twig a flimsy spray . . .
Still   who can tell?   The branch may not break but
     like a
fiberglass wand bearing far more than its own weight
pull us all together to a temporary
clearing   the sky making both sense
and beauty   the high-pitched stars singing their
     linked songs
the trees calling also   *We have meaning   meaning*:
the animals staring with large reflective eyes . . .

                              (first published in *Kalliope*)

(This, I should point out, is a syllabic poem, in which
all the lines have twelve syllables, except for the fifth line
of each stanza, which has eight. I worked it out this way
in order to highlight Yeats's line and its music: "And the
white breast of the dim sea.")

One final note on this subject. Just because I believe
that poems should reach out for truth and meaning,
doesn't mean I believe you have to write "rational" or
"traditional" poetry—though I *do* believe that contemporary poetry in general could do with greater clarity, and
more generosity, toward its readers. As Adrienne Rich
has pointed out, "Too much already has been buried,
mystified, or written of necessity in code."

4) *We want to make something beautiful.* This last
major reason is perhaps the most important. It's also the
most frustrating.

Our lives often feel as if they're spinning out of control, certainly out of *our* control. But art in general, and
writing poetry in particular, can give us the illusion of
being able to make something perfect. For a little while,

we can work on a project, set its parameters, decide everything about it.

I think we're at our best when we're writing poetry. We're in our most selfless, least selfish state. We truly want to do something good. That shouldn't be too hard. "All a poem is," X. J. Kennedy has said, "is an emotionally disturbing structure made of words."

But, "the best words," in the "best order": There's the rub. Which are they? Time after time, the poet kneels in his patch of words. "Between my finger and my thumb / The squat pen rests," writes Seamus Heaney. "I'll dig with it."

The perfect poem may be an illusion, but each time you face a blank page (or screen), the possibility exists, and you start again. Like Charlie Brown about to kick the football before his muse, Lucy, yanks it away, we begin over and over with fresh paper and hope.

And what's the result? Well, that's not entirely for us to say, is it? Some critics, editors, teachers, friends will say one thing; some will say another. You should listen. You should study. You should read. And then you should start writing again.

A long time ago, at the Minneapolis Museum of Art, I went to an exhibition of Marsden Hartley's paintings of shore birds. Hartley was a good friend of William Carlos Williams, and he also wrote poetry, often on the backs of his paintings (reproduced in the exhibit), as he tried to capture the beauty of the birds in every possible way he could. This effort was very moving to me, and resulted, some time later, in a poem called "Plovers," first published in the *South Florida Review*. This is its—and this book's—conclusion:

. . . Someday a poem of mine snapping across the
white reaches of blank space just ahead of the

blind sea in which all is lost may swing
   around the bend clickety-clack and find
   chuckling unaware that golden plover O rare
   shining in glorious sunlight unafraid
   around its neck a silver clasp with a poem
   of Hartley's rolled inside head & back erect
   on long quick legs and will run around
      over & through it eyes wings beak will be mine
      the poem will cradle that bird & protect
         and caress those unbelievable soft feathers &
      frail bone
and will take it all alone to Cape Cod
      or Narragansett an abandoned beach
on a rainy day by the cold sea
and there I suppose
will give it back to Hartley & it will be
a feather in the golden cap of God

ℬ. 16

A Glossary

F INALLY, HERE'S a glossary of most of the terms that I've mentioned in this book so far, plus a few more. Some excellent detailed guides are Alex Preminger's *The Princeton Handbook of Poetic Terms*, Philip Jason's and Allan Lefcowitz's *Creative Writing Handbook*, and C. Hugh Holman and William Harmon's *A Handbook to Literature*, among many others.

abecedarian: a type of acrostic in which the lines begin, in order, with the letters of the alphabet (e.g., "The ABC of Aerobics")

accentual verse: lines in which you count only the major beats or accents, but not the number of syllables (e.g., G. M. Hopkins's "The Windhover," which begins: "I <u>caught</u> this <u>morn</u>ing <u>morn</u>ing's min<u>ion</u>, <u>king</u>- / dom of <u>day</u>light's <u>dau</u>phin, dapple-<u>dawn</u>-drawn <u>Fal</u>con, in his <u>rid</u>ing . . ."

accentual-alliterative verse: accentual verse based on old Germanic prosody where typically two of the beats in the first half of the line have the same initial consonant as one in the second half (e.g., W. H. Auden's "The Age of Anxiety": "How <u>well</u> and <u>witty</u> when you <u>wake</u> up, / How <u>glad</u> and <u>good</u> when you <u>go</u> to bed, /

Do you <u>feel</u>, my <u>friend?</u> What <u>fla</u>vour has / That <u>liq</u>uor you <u>lift</u> with your <u>left</u> hand?")

accentual-syllabic verse: the standard measurement of formal poetry in English, where both the number of accents and the number of syllables are counted; the *pattern* of these forms the meter (e.g., iambic tetrameter means a line with four iambic feet: "where <u>men</u> may <u>sit</u> and con<u>template</u>")

acrostic: a poem in which the first letters of each line spell out a name or some meaningful word when read downward (e.g., François Villon's "Ballade to His Mistress")

alliteration: a repetition of beginning consonant sounds (e.g., "some strung-out stranger")

allusion: a brief reference to something, usually mythological, literary or historic, that may enrich the poem (e.g., the reference to Dr. Johnson in "Apples")

anapestic foot: a poetic foot with three syllables: two unaccented followed by one accented (e.g., "in my <u>life</u>" or "repro<u>duce</u>")

assonance: repetition of similar vowel sounds (e.g., "scars like my father's")

ballad: a narrative poem usually told in quatrains rhyming ABCB (e.g., W. H. Auden's "Miss Gee" and "Victor")

ballade: a French form consisting of three eight-line stanzas rhyming ababbcbC and a four-line envoy rhyming bcbC (e.g., François Villon's famous "Ballade of the Ladies of Times Gone By")

blank verse: unrhymed iambic pentameter (e.g., "When I saw birches in Wasienki Park / leaning against the wind   I thought of you / old ghost   so strongly have you claimed those trees . . .")

caesura: a rhetorical pause within the poetic line (e.g., "This was the fifties   life could be shocking then")

cinquain: a five-line unrhymed syllabic poem, the lines consisting of two, four, six, eight, and two syllables, respectively (e.g., "The Soul," by Babette Deutsch, p. 95)

cliche: a trite, overused phrase or idea (e.g., "good as gold")

coda: concluding part of a poem that summarizes its idea (e.g., many of the couplets at the end of Shakespeare's sonnets: "So long as men can breathe, or eyes can see, / So long lives this, and this gives life to thee.")

conceit: an elaborate, ingenious, and extended image, often used by metaphysical poets like John Donne (e.g., comparing his bed to the world in "The Sun Rising")

consonance: repetition of similar consonants around different vowels (e.g., "pauper / paper / piper" or "rate / right /root")

couplet: a two-line stanza, often rhymed (e.g., "Nature, and Nature's laws, lay hid in night: / God said, *Let Newton be!* and all was light.")

dactylic foot: a poetic foot with three syllables: one accented followed by two unaccented (e.g., "<u>fee</u>ling it" or "<u>Anna</u>bel")

dimeter: a line of two feet (e.g. "<u>learn</u>ing too <u>late</u> / he <u>hat</u>ed small <u>feet</u> / but <u>such</u> is our <u>lot</u>: / You <u>can't</u> escape <u>fate</u>")

double dactyl: two dactylic feet in a row (e.g., "<u>What</u> if a <u>much</u> of a . . .")

elegy: a meditation on death or a lament for the dead (e.g., Dylan Thomas's "A Refusal to Mourn the Death, by Fire, of a Child in London")

English (or Shakespearean) sonnet: a sonnet typically rhyming ababcdcd efefgg (e.g., Marilyn Nelson's
"Chopin")

end rhyme: rhyme at the ends of lines (e.g., "In my criminal stage I fell in love with <u>Bert</u> / who did an awkward handstand in her <u>skirt</u>")

end-stopped lines: lines that end with a pause, often
marked by punctuation (e.g., "A little learning is a
dang'rous <u>thing;</u> / Drink deep, or taste not the Pierian
<u>spring</u>")

enjambment: lines that continue, or "run on," to the
next line without an end-stop (e.g., "In winter even
their / parents eatthem as they flick / back and
forth . . .")

envoy (sometimes **envoi**): a short concluding stanza, as
the three-line ending of a sestina or the four-line ending of a ballade

epic: a lengthy narrative poem with a hero, such as
Homer's *Odyssey*, along with its opposite, the **mock-
epic** like Alexander Pope's "The Rape of the Lock,"
which treats a silly subject grandiosely and satirically

foot: a syllabic group forming a basic rhythmical unit
(e.g. an iambic *foot*)

free verse: poetry without a set pattern of rhyme or
meter

half rhyme (or near, off, or slant rhyme): rhyme that
relies on assonance or consonance for its effects (e.g.
"road / ride" or "fall / cool" or "candle / swindle"—
rather than **true rhyme** like "road / code" or "fall /
call" or "candle / handle"

haiku: a seventeen-syllable Japanese poem traditionally
consisting of three lines with five, seven, and five syl-

lables respectively, treating a subject with natural imagery and symbolic or emotional content

heptameter: a line of seven feet (e.g. Rudyard Kipling's "Oh, East is East, and West is West, and never the twain shall meet . . .")

hexameter: a line of six feet (e.g., Howard Nemerov's "Why are the stamps adorned with kings and presidents? / That we may lick their hinder parts and thump their heads.")

hyperbole: exaggeration for an effect (e.g., "a sentence filled a room with dead birds")

iambic foot: a poetic foot with two syllables, one unaccented followed by one accented (e.g. "a girl" or "machine" or "they laughed")

iambic pentameter: the most common formal line in English poetry, consisting of five iambic feet (e.g., "And yet my love our love's as quick to kindle / as simpler loves if love were ever simple")

internal rhyme: rhyme within the line (e.g., "this was hard but ripeness is all / proclaimeth the bard")

inversion: placing words out of their normal order for effect, as in Milton's "Long is the way / and hard, that out of hell leads up to light")

Italian (or Petrarchan) sonnet: a sonnet typically rhyming abbaabba cdecde or cdcdcd (e.g., Keats's "On First Looking Into Chapman's Homer")

lyric: generally a short personal poem that emphasizes its sound or music, as compared to narrative or epic poetry (e.g., Theodore Roethke's "I Knew A Woman")

metaphor: a direct comparison between different things (e.g., "You're a rat" or "my heart's ink")

metaphysical: a type of poetry most prominent in the

seventeenth century, marked by ingenuity and intri-
cacy, typically using the device of the **conceit,** an
elaborate and ingenious image (e.g. John Donne's
"The Flea," where a flea biting Donne's mistress becomes a symbol of their love)

meter: a measurable rhythmic pattern, as in iambic pentameter

modernism: a revolutionary movement in the arts, generally placed between the World Wars, that favored
experimentation over tradition (e.g., most famously
in poetry, T. S. Eliot's "The Waste Land" or Ezra
Pound's "Cantos")

monometer: a line of one foot (e.g., David Baker's "Sonnet for a Separation": "Where have / you gone, / my
love? / Moon on / our wet / street burns / without /
you . . ."

neoclassical: a type of poetry most prominent in the
eighteenth century, marked by moderation, common
sense, and wit, typically using rhymed couplets and
other balanced forms, as in the work of John Dryden,
Samuel Johnson, Jonathan Swift, and Alexander
Pope.

occasional poetry: poetry written for a specific occasion
(e.g., a poem for a president's inauguration or a royal
wedding, etc.)

octameter: a line of eight feet (e.g. Edgar Allan Poe's
"The Raven": "Suddenly I heard a tapping, as of someone gently rapping . . ."

octave: a stanza of eight lines

octet: the first eight lines of a traditional sonnet

ode: an elaborate lyric, usually exalting or praising the
subject (e.g., Keats's "Ode to a Nightingale" or Shelley's "Ode to the West Wind")

off-rhyme: see *half-rhyme*

onomatopoeia: words and syllables that recreate the sounds of the object described (e.g. "The moan of doves in immemorial elms, / And murmuring of innumerable bees," from Tennyson's "Come Down, O Maid")

ottava rima: an eight-line stanza, usually in iambic pentameter, rhyming abababcc (e.g., Byron's *Don Juan* and Yeats's "Among School Children")

oxymoron: a linkage of contradictory words (e.g., "sweet cruelty," "cool fever," "towering pygmy")

pantoum: a Malayan form of indefinite length, in quatrains, where the second and fourth lines of each quatrain are repeated as the first and third lines of the following quatrain; in the last quatrain the first and third line of the poem are repeated in reverse order, so the poem begins and ends with the same line (e.g., "Atomic Pantoum")

parallelism: repeated rhythms or structures (e.g., "Out of the cradle endlessly rocking, / Out of the mockingbird's throat, the musical shuttle . . .")

paradox: a self-contradictory statement that might nevertheless be true (e.g., Shelley's "To a Skylark": "Our sincerest laughter / with some pain is fraught")

parody: a caricature, usually humorous, of a serious poem or poetic style (e.g., Henry Reed's send-up of T. S. Eliot, which begins, "As we get older we do not get any younger . . .")

pastoral: a poem celebrating nature and rural life, often featuring shepherds and shepherdesses (e.g., Wordsworth's "Michael")

pentameter: a line of five feet (e.g., "I swallow all things up like Aaron's rod")

personification: giving human qualities to non-human

things (e.g. "Chicken Unlimited worries about his
input / he wants to make it perfectly clear . . .")
prose poem: a poem that is printed like prose, in para-
graphs instead of stanzas, but using other traditional
poetic devices (e.g., poems by Russell Edson, Jim Car-
roll and others)
prosody: the study of the metrical structure of poetry
pyrrhic foot: a poetic foot with two unaccented syllables
(e.g. "of a" or "in the")

quatrain: a four-line stanza, rhymed or unrhymed (e.g.,
Wilbur's "Museum Piece")
quintain: a five-line stanza, rhymed or unrhymed (e.g.,
the tanka or limerick or John Crowe Ransom's "Philo-
mela"

refrain: a regularly repeated line, phrase, or stanza
(e.g., Dylan Thomas's "Rage, rage, against the dying
of the light.")
renga: a linking of the tanka form into a series, often
done in collaboration with other poets, popularized by
the Mexican poet Octavio Paz and his friends
repeton: a repeated line that is not a refrain, as in the
repeated lines of pantoums
rhyme: the repetition of the same or similar sounds
rhythm: an ordered and recurring movement in the poetic line, whether measurable in metric feet (meter)
or in free verse
romanticism: a literary movement of the nineteenth
century, rebelling against neoclassical poetry,
marked by greater stylistic freedom, a love of nature
and exotic places, with an emphasis on the individual
(e.g., Wordsworth, Shelley, Coleridge, Whitman, etc.)
rondeau: a French form (it means "little circle") consisting of fifteen lines, divided into a quintain (aabba), a

quatrain (aabR), and a sestet (aabbaR); "R"—the refrain—echoes part of the first line, and there are only
two rhymes (e.g., Marilyn Hacker's "Rondeau After a
Transatlantic Telephone Call")

run-on line: see enjambment

satire: a poem that ridicules a person, institution, or society, with the intention of reforming or diminishing
it (e.g., Howard Nemerov's "Boom!")

scansion: a system for analyzing, measuring, or scan-
ning poetry (e.g., underlining or adding accents to indicate stressed syllables, etc.)

sestet: a six-line stanza or the last six lines of a traditional sonnet

sestina: a 39-line poem consisting of six sestets and a
three-line envoy; the end-words of the first six lines
are repeated in a set pattern: see Chapter 9 (e.g, Elizabeth Bishop's "Sestina")

simile: a comparison between different things, using
"like" or "as" or "as if" (e.g., "O, my Luve's like a red
red rose")

sonnet: a fourteen-line poem, usually written in iambic
pentameter and divided into an octet and sestet, with
various rhyme schemes (e.g., Archibald MacLeish's
"The End of the World")

spondee: a poetic foot of two accented syllables (e.g.,
"What luck!" or "Blow, blow . . .")

stanza: separate groups of lines in poems, of varying
length and formality

stress: an accented or emphasized syllable or sound (e.g.
in "major" the stress is on the first syllable)

surrealism: in poetry, irrational or unrelated images
and structure, common in twentieth-century poetry
and related to *modernism* (e.g., Caroline Knox's "The

Crybaby at the Library," in which a student's tears
literally—or surreally—flood the library)

syllabics or syllabic meter: poems whose line length is
decided by syllable count: see Chapter 8 (e.g., "Goalfish")

symbol: an object or image that stands for something
else (e.g., the "Tree" in "The Golden Bird," standing
for pure imagination)

tanka: a 31-syllable Japanese poem consisting of five
lines of 5/7/5/7/7 syllables respectively (e.g., Steven
Lautermilch's sequence, "Petals on a Burning Pond")

teleuton: the end-word of a line, especially one that is
repeated, as in a sestina

tercet or triplet: a three-line stanza, rhymed or unrhymed (e.g., William Carlos Williams's "The Yachts")

terza rima: interlocked tercets rhyming aba bcb cdc, etc.
(e.g., Dante's *The Divine Comedy* and Shelley's "Ode
to the West Wind")

tetrameter: a line of four feet (e.g., "There the trees are
cool and dark / and men may sit and contemplate /
the myriad forms that love can take . . .")

trimeter: a line of three feet (e.g., Roethke's "My Papa's
Waltz": "The whiskey on your breath / Could make a
small boy dizzy . . .")

trochaic foot: a poetic foot of two syllables, the first accented and the second unaccented (e.g., "Venus" or
"greeneyed . . ."

true rhyme: repetition of identical sounds (e.g., "house"
and "mouse")

villanelle: a nineteen-line poem rhyming aba aba aba
aba abaabaa, with the first and third lines repeating
in a set pattern: see Chapter 11 (e.g., Dylan Thomas's
"Do Not Go Gentle Into That Good Night")

Selected Bibliography

Abse, Dannie. *A Strong Dose of Myself.* Hutchinson & Co. (London), 1983.

Barfield, Owen. *Poetic Diction: A Study in Meaning.* McGraw-Hill, Inc., 1964.

Bender, Sheila, ed. *The Writer's Journal.* Dell Publishing, 1997.

Boswell, James. *Life of Johnson.* Viking Penguin, 1979.

Corn, Alfred. *The Poem's Heartbeat.* Story Line Press, 1997.

Dacey, Philip & Jauss, David, eds. *Strong Measures: Contemporary Poetry in Traditional Forms.* Addison-Wesley Educ. Pub., 1989.

Dodd, Wayne. *Toward the End of the Century.* U. of Iowa Press, 1992.

Gioia, Dana. *Can Poetry Matter?* Graywolf Press, 1992.

Gross, Harvey & McDowell, Robert. *Sound and Form in Modern Poetry.* U. of Michigan Press, 1996.

Hall, Donald. *Life Work.* Beacon Press, 1993.

———. *Their Ancient Glittering Eyes.* Ticknor & Fields, 1992,

Harmon, William & Holman, Hugh, eds. *A Handbook to Literature.* Prentice Hall, 1995.

Heaney, Seamus. *Preoccupations.* Faber & Faber, 1984.

Hofstadter, Douglas. *Godel, Escher, Bach.* Vintage Books, 1980.

Hollander, John. *Rhyme's Reason.* Yale U. Press, 1981.

Hugo, Richard. *The Triggering Town.* W.W. Norton, 1979.

Jarman, Mark & Mason, David, eds. *Rebel Angels.* Story Line Press, 1996.

Jason, Philip & Lefcowitz, Allen, eds. *Creative Writer's Handbook.* Prentice Hall, 1990.

Kalstone, David. *Becoming a Poet.* Noonday Press, 1989.

Keats, John. *Selected Poems and Letters.* The Riverside Press, 1959.

Kinzie, Mary. *The Cure of Poetry in an Age of Prose.* U. of Chicago Press, 1993.

Kirby, David. *Writing Poetry.* The Writer, Inc., 1997.

Koch, Kenneth. *The Art of Poetry.* U. of Michigan Press, 1996.

Kuusisto, Stephen; Tall, Deborah; & Weiss, David, eds. *The Poet's Notebook,* 1995.

Lamman, Martin, ed. *Written in Water, Written in Stone: Twenty Years of Poets on Poetry.* U. of Michigan Press, 1996.

McCauley, James. *Versification.* Michigan State U. Press, 1996.

Myers, Jack & Simms, Michael, eds. *Longman's Dictionary of Poetic Terms.* Longman Group of the U.K., 1989.

Nemerov, Howard. *Figures of Thought.* David R. Godine, 1978.

———. *Reflexions on Poetry & Poetics.* Rutgers U. Press, 1972.

Nims, John Frederick, ed. *Western Wind.* McGraw-Hill, Inc., 1992.

Packard, William, ed. *The Craft of Poetry.* Doubleday & Co., 1974.

Perrine, Laurence. *Sound and Sense.* Harcourt Brace Jovanovich, Inc. 1977.

Pinsky, Robert. *The Sounds of Poetry.* Farrar, Straus & Giroux, 1998.

Rich, Adrienne. *On Lies, Secrets, and Silence*. W.W. Norton & Co., 1979.

Rilke, Rainer Maria. *Letters to a Young Poet*. W.W. Norton & Co., 1962.

Rosenberg, Philip, ed. *Tygers of Wrath*. St. Martin's Press, 1992.

Rico, Gabriele. *Writing the Natural Way*. J.P. Tarcher Pub., 1983.

Rukeyser, Muriel. *The Life of Poetry*. Wm. Morrow & Co., 1949.

Simpson, Louis. *The Character of the Poet*. U. of Michigan Press, 1986.

Thompson, John. *The Founding of English Meter*. Columbia U. Press, 1989.

Turco, Lewis. *The Book of Forms*. E.P. Dutton, 1968.

Wallace, Robert & Boisseau, Michelle, eds. *Writing Poems*. HarperCollins, 1995.